Francophone Women Writers of Africa and the Caribbean

Francophone Women Writers of Africa and the Caribbean

Renée Larrier

University Press of Florida
Gainesville · Tallahassee · Tampa · Boca Raton
Pensacola · Orlando · Miami · Jacksonville

Copyright 2000 by the Board of Regents of the State of Florida
Printed in the United States of America on acid-free paper
All rights reserved

05 04 03 02 01 00 6 5 4 3 2 1

Library of Congress Cataloging-in-Publication Data

Larrier, Renée Brenda.
Francophone women writers of Africa and the Caribbean /
Renée Larrier.
p. cm.
Includes bibliographical references.
ISBN 0-8130-1742-4 (alk. paper)
1. African literature (French)—Women authors—History and
criticism. 2. Caribbean literature (French)—Women authors—
History and criticism. 3. Women and literature—Africa. 4.
Women and literature—West Indies, French. I. Title.
PQ3980.5 .L36 2000
840.9'9287—dc21 99-056589

The University Press of Florida is the scholarly publishing agency
for the State University System of Florida, comprising Florida
A&M University, Florida Atlantic University, Florida
International University, Florida State University, University of
Central Florida, University of Florida, University of North
Florida, University of South Florida, and University of West
Florida.

University Press of Florida
15 Northwest 15th Street
Gainesville, FL 32611–2079
http://www.upf.com

For my mother, Naomi, and my sister, Diane

Contents

Acknowledgments

I wish to thank the Rutgers University Faculty Academic Study Program and French Department for granting me a timely sabbatical to research and write this book, and the Center for Latin American Studies at the University of Florida where a Rockefeller Humanist-in-Residence Fellowship allowed me the time and space to conceive chapter 3.

The contributions of scholars/friends and family can never be underestimated. I am indebted to Brinda Mehta for her insightful comments on an early version of the manuscript and to Janis A. Mayes for her astute suggestions, especially concerning the translations. I am also grateful to the anonymous readers at the University Press of Florida for their guidance in strengthening the manuscript and to editor Susan Fernandez for her enthusiasm and commitment to this project.

Most of all, I would like to acknowledge the invaluable support over the years of friends Carol Cherry, Francine Essien, Signithia Fordham, and Cheryl Wall, and the consistent and unwavering encouragement of my parents Naomi and Marvin Larrier, sister Diane Collier, nephew Matthew Noel and niece Melanie Blisse, as well as aunt Gracelia Carter and brother-in-law Bernard Collier, who left us too soon.

Introduction

Inscriptions of Women's Voices
Female Authority in Francophone Africa and the Caribbean

> It is perhaps the great discomfort of those trying to silence the world to discover that we have voices sealed inside our heads, voices that with each passing day grow even louder than the clamor of the world outside.
>
> **Edwidge Danticat, *The Farming of Bones***

> Je suis qui tu ignores . . .
> Et voici que je romps les chaînes,
> et le silence menteur
> Que tu jetas sur moi
>
> (I am whom you don't know . . .
> And now I am breaking the chains
> And the fallacious silence
> That you cast on me)
>
> **Ndèye Coumba Mbengue Diakhaté**

"Et pourtant, comme elles ont à dire et à écrire!" (and yet what things they have to tell and to write!) is the way in which prize-winning Senegalese novelist Mariama Bâ formulated the gap between the paucity of African women writers and the large number of stories they had to tell ("Fonction" 6). Since 1981, however, when Bâ first made that statement, and as we approach the new millennium, there has been a virtual explosion of activity as African women along with African American and Caribbean women have sold an unprecedented number of novels, short stories, poems, plays, and autobiographies. Mariama Bâ's association of women telling and writing intimates voice and inscription, respectively. Inscribing female voices, which signifies the authors' own orality as well as their characters', is an effective way of articulating women's perspectives on issues that concern them. That francophone African and Caribbean women writers often create first-person female narrators who relate their own story produces dual authorship or "double *auteur(ité)*," so to speak. While the tension between these two voices is not the focus of this study, my point is that double-voiced enunciation is one way women writers wrest the representation of their experiences from others. It also moves them—writers and characters—toward subjectivity, empowering them, thus conferring authority on women and their communities.

Francophone Women Writers of Africa and the Caribbean embraces Clémentine Faik-Nzuji's *Symboles graphiques en Afrique noire* in which she demonstrates the importance in oral cultures of graphic symbols that are traced, sculpted, engraved, scarified, drawn, painted, encrusted, tattooed, or woven (61). These symbols convey messages, function as a language, and can be considered comparable to letters on a page. I argue that women can and do inscribe their voice on various sites, in Wolof, in Creole, in Bassa, on paper in French.

Authority is a key term in this work. I am referring at once to women as authors; but just as important, I am borrowing the sense of the term from the Société Africaine de Culture in the introduction to *La civilisation de la femme dans la tradition africaine* in which "autorité et compétence de la femme dans la gestion de la vie familiale et sociale" (authority and competence of the woman in the management of family and social life) is one of the topics the collection of essays addresses (14). Authority in this context denotes power in certain gendered domains, within the specific locations of the family and social life. In this study, I would like to broaden the purview of women's authority to include writing by francophone women of African descent.

What do women tell or say when they write? What are their concerns? What are the sources of their stories? *Francophone Women Writers of Africa and the Caribbean* explores the various ways in which women's voices are inscribed, closely analyzing representative texts—from text(iles) to initiation tales, novels, and life stories. I argue that francophone African and Caribbean women writers through twofold authorship/"double *auteur(ité)*" reappropriate their orality—that is, voices that had been usurped by others—in order to transmit knowledge. In so doing, they challenge constructions of women and their experiences found in orature, literature, and popular culture.

Women's voices transmit knowledge, culture, and wisdom.[1] Trinh T. Minh-ha's crediting of women's memories as "the world's earliest archives or libraries," which extends Amadou Hampaté Bâ's claim about male traditionalists (121),[2] implies that women through their voices are one repository of history, a history which has systematically marginalized their contributions. Furthermore, African and Caribbean women's perspectives are largely overlooked in the theoretical formulations of négritude, créolité, and the Black Atlantic. The absence of women from discussions of *créolité*, a popular topic in Caribbean intellectual circles, is as striking as their virtual absence from Paul Gilroy's concept of the Black Atlantic. I whole-heartedly agree with Juliana Makuchi Nfah-Abbenyi's position in *Gender in African Women's Writing: Identity, Sexuality, and Difference* (1997) that theory should emerge from the texts themselves; that is, the authors give the reader clues as to how to approach their works. I would like to suggest that francophone African and Caribbean women writers' propen-sity for women-centered/woman-narrated texts is significant in itself and should be addressed.

In my investigation, I read across the francophone African diaspora, pairing an African and a Caribbean text, a methodology justified in part by the common experiences of gender, slavery, and colonization, which also means these authors do not write in their mother tongue. Carole Boyce Davies makes two significant points in favor of reading across the diaspora in *Black Women, Writing, and Identity: Migrations of the Subject*. For one, she posits that black women's writing "re-connects and re-members, brings together black women dis-located by space and time" (4). Second, her notion of "migratory subjectivities," the repositioning of identities which results when writers relocate, is relevant to francophone African and Caribbean writers. Guadeloupeans Maryse Condé lives in New York, Myriam Warner-Vieyra is a longtime resident of Senegal, and Jocelyn Etienne spent many years in Côte d'Ivoire; Haitian-born Marie Chauvet, Edwidge Danticat, Marlène Rigaud Apollon, and Liliane Desvieux settled in New York, Brooklyn, Baltimore, and Canada, respectively. French-born Gisèle Pineau moved to Guadeloupe; Ivorian Véronique Tadjo lives in Kenya; Cameroonian Werewere Liking works out of Côte d'Ivoire; and Haitian Micheline Dusseck is published in Barcelona; Michèle Maillet migrated to France from Martinique.

While this study is also positioned as a series of boundary crossings, I am not denying the specificity of national cultures and literatures, a fear Chandra Talpade Mohanty and Adrien Huannou express strongly. Never-theless, the slave trade brought West Africans to the Caribbean, where new societies were formed and, to this day, the African component in Creole culture remains very strong. At the same time, however, African cultures are neither monolithic nor static. They continue to evolve over time. Still, despite the geographical distance and national, ethnic, religious, and lan-guage differences that separate these writers from Cameroon, Guadeloupe, Haiti, Mali, Martinique, and Senegal, all countries with strong literary traditions, their works share common thematic and discursive threads. My objective is to contribute to the growing critical discourse on women's writing, which has not yet fully considered this perspective.

The concern about achieving voice through authorship for black women cross-culturally, to borrow Filomena Steady's term, spans generations. Calixthe Beyala from Cameroon, who was born thirty years after Mariama Bâ and published eight novels between 1987 and 1998, declares unequivocally in *Amina*: "J'avais des choses à dire, alors je me suis mise à écrire" (I had things to say, so I began to write) (85). Haitian poet Erma Saint-Grégoire became an author "mostly because I have something to say" (463), a sentiment echoed in the title of African American centenarians Sarah L. and A. Elizabeth Delany's autobiography *Having Our Say: The Delany Sisters' First Hundred Years*.

The women's literary explosion in francophone Africa and the Caribbean is, in part, an outgrowth of the historical and cultural phenomenon of the 1970s, which witnessed the unparalleled interest in women globally. From the United Nations' declaration of "the Decade of the Woman," the 1972 conference in Abidjan, Côte d'Ivoire, titled "La civilisation de la femme dans la tradition africaine," the UN closing conference in Nairobi, to the Beijing Fourth World Conference on Women in 1995, women became, for a while, the center of attention. It was within this global context, in part, that two publications in French celebrating the extraordinary achievements of African women and those of the diaspora appeared. The six-volume multiauthored *Femmes: Livre d'or de la femme créole* (1989) chronicles the presence of women in the Caribbean, from early Amerindians to present-day political leaders and artists.[3] Simone Schwarz-Bart's six-volume encyclopedia *Hommage à la femme noire* (1988–89) is broader in scope, balancing photographs, paintings, sculptures, engravings, lithographs, and short biographies of historical figures with numerous interspersed "paroles d'une femme ordinaire" (words of an ordinary woman). These women's voices illustrate Schwarz-Bart's resolve to allow women whom history ignores, whose opinions are rarely solicited, and whose voices are seldom inscribed the opportunity to have their say. In her encyclopedia Schwarz-Bart shows the ways in which women of African descent are represented as well as the ways in which they represent themselves.

In the 1970s discussions about women coincided with French-speaking African and Caribbean women writers making their mark on the literary scene, a trajectory Aminata Sow Fall characterizes as "du pilon à la machine à écrire" (from the pestle to the typewriter), and Irène Assiba d'Almeida calls a "prise d'écriture" (taking of writing) (6). Not only did these women writers take advantage of new opportunities and access to publishers,[4] over the years many have received recognition in the form of literary awards for their efforts.[5]

Francophone African and Caribbean women's writings, along with those of their anglophone, hispanophone, and lusophone sisters, are read transnationally and analyzed in venues ranging from college and university classrooms to two first-time public forums. For example, at the Salon des Écrivaines Africaines Sub-sahariennes, writers, critics, and teachers gathered at the Université de Ouagadougou, Burkina Faso, in December 1998. In New York, in October 1997, the Organization of Women Writers of Africa convened "Yari Yari Black Women Writers and the Future," where hundreds of writers, such as Ama Ata Aidoo, Nancy Morejón, Nawal El Saadawi, Maya Angelou, Octavia Butler, Buchi Emecheta, Lorna Goodison, Gisèle Pineau, Jayne Cortez, Aminata Sow Fall, Sonia Sanchez, Angela Davis, Edwidge Danticat, Véronique Tadjo, Louise Meriwether, Micere Mugo, gave readings, talked about their work, and participated on panels with academics. Scholarly associations such as the African Literature Association, which regularly holds panels on women's writings, dedicated its 1991 conference to the theme of *nwanyibu,* or "womanbeing," and subsequently published the proceedings;[6] the Association of Caribbean Women Writers and Scholars held its biannual conference in Grenada in May 1998. The above-mentioned organizations and conferences are complemented by various projects aimed at documenting women's literary production.[7] That there is a school in Dakar named after Nafissatou Diallo, one on Gorée Island named after Mariama Bâ, and there exist websites devoted to francophone African and Caribbean women writers attest to the popularity and appreciation of their work as well.

While writing among francophone African and Caribbean women is often perceived as a late-twentieth-century phenomenon, the contributions of female literary artists began much earlier. For one, Virginie Sampeur's poems and short stories appeared in various nineteenth-century Haitian magazines, followed by Ida Faubert, whose poems appeared in *Haïti littéraire et scientique.*[8] Ten years prior to the publication of her more well-known novel *Le Joug* in 1934, Annie Desroy's play *Et l'amour vient* was performed. Cléanthes Valcin published two novels in 1929, *Cruelle destinée* and *La blanche négresse.* Marie Chauvet's play *La légende des fleurs* dates from 1949. Although not as old or established as Haiti's female literary tradition, Martinique counts among its early writers Paulette Nardal, who published short stories in the early decades of this century, and Suzanne Césaire, who cofounded the journal *Tropiques* in 1940. While the collaboration between Claude and Marie-Magdeleine Carbet produced several prose works prior to 1950, Marie-Magdeleine subsequently published a dozen volumes of poetry and prose on her own.[9] Senegalese poet Annette Mbaye d'Erneville, who began publishing during the 1950s, founded *Awa* in 1963, the first magazine by and for francophone African women. In 1964 she was one of the founders of the Association des Écrivains du Sénégal. All of these women inscribed their own voices and those of other women. Furthermore, there exists a body of texts in oral form (songs, poems, lullabies, proverbs, narratives—in short, orature) that has and continues to inform their written texts.

The complex link between oral and written narratives in Africa and the Caribbean has been established by critics such as Yves Emmanuel Dogbé in *La tradition orale source de la littérature contemporaine en Afrique* (1985); Amadou Koné in *Du récit oral au roman: Étude sur les avatars de la tradition héroïque dans le roman africain* (1985); Ngugi wa Thiongo in *Decolonising the Mind* (1986); Maximilien Laroche in *La double scène de la représentation: Oraliture et littérature dans la Caraïbe* (1991); Isidore Okpewho in *African Oral Literature: Backgrounds, Character and Continuity* (1992); Nora-Alexandra Kazi-Tani in *Roman africain de langue française au carrefour de l'écrit et de l'oral* (1995); and Eileen Julien in *African Novels and the Question of Orality* (1992). Julien challenges the idea that oral/written modes are hierarchical, sequential. These critics, however, use male writers to support their claim.

Women's inscriptions of orality extend beyond the incorporation of oral forms and even beyond the discourse enunciated by Edouard Glissant in *Le discours antillais* (1981), whose personal approach to writing in French is consistent with the technique of many other recent authors: "J'évoque une synthèse, synthèse de la syntaxe écrite et de la rythmique parlée, de l'«acquis» d'écriture et du 'réflexe' oral, de la solitude d'écriture et de la participation au chanter commun" (I am referring to a synthesis, synthesis of written syntax and spoken rhythms, of "acquired" writing and oral "reflex," of the solitude of writing and the solidarity of the collective voice) (256/147). Francophone women's writings embrace woman-centered/woman-*narrated* texts, from Annette Mbaye d'Erneville's transcribed lullaby/poem "Berceuse," to Simone Schwarz-Bart's inscription of Marie-Ange's voice on audiocassette in her play *Ton Beau Capitaine* (1987), to the novels and life stories that form the foundation of this study.

Francophone African and Caribbean women writers reclaim sites of inscription for women in societies where they often pass unacknowledged as storytellers. In Caribbean cultures such *conteurs* are almost always figured as male. Although contemporary fiction writer Patrick Chamoiseau bemoans the gradual disappearance of *conteurs* in *Solibo magnifique,* he assures that their legacy will not be forgotten by centering a novel on one of them. Likewise, Raphaël Confiant guarantees their visibility with his *Les maîtres de la parole créole* (1995), a collection of twenty-six interviews with "masters of the Creole word" from Martinique, Guadeloupe, Haiti, Dominica, French Guiana, and St. Lucia, each name supported by a short biography, photograph, and a transcribed and translated story. The legacy of these *conteurs* is thus secured in written form. Moreover, narratives in which an African or Caribbean storyteller figures as a character suggest that the trade is gender specific: the above-mentioned *Solibo magnifique,* Mamadou Kouyaté in Djibril Tamsir Niane's *Sounjata ou l'épopée mandingue,* Amadou Koumba in Birago Diop's *Les contes d'Amadou Koumba* (Tales of Amadou Koumba), Médouze in Zobel's *La rue cases-nègres* (Black Shack Alley), Antoine in Jacques Roumain's *Gouverneurs de la rosée* (Masters of the Dew), Maître Honorien in Raphaël Confiant's *Ravines du devant-jour,* Cyrille in Maryse Condé's *Traversée de la man-grove* (Crossing the Mangrove), and Papa Longoué in several of Edouard Glissant's novels.[10] Ironically, Birago Diop mentions that he heard some of the tales that form his collection from his grandmother, and Dany Laferrière fondly recalls that his grandmother would tell him stories as a boy: "Da me racontera toutes sortes d'histoires de zombies, de loups-garous et de diablesses jusqu'à ce que je m'endorme" (Da told me all sorts of stories about zombies, werewolves, and "diablesses" until I fell asleep) (20). Chamoiseau's Solibo magnifique, renowned for his ability with words, learned the art of storytelling from his mother. What accounts then, for the quasi absence of women storytellers from prominent positions in these texts? Why do these writers not do a better job of formally celebrat-ing female antecedents? As history relegates women's experiences to the margins in many other domains, storytelling is likewise depicted as a mas-culine endeavor.

Jean-Marie Adiaffi from Côte d'Ivoire cites another sphere of gender-specific orality and its inscription. In his novel *La carte d'identité,* he iden-tifies the drum as an important site of inscription, and thus the drummer is figured as a writer. According to Adiaffi, both the instrument and the musician speak a sacred language that is passed down from generation to generation:

tam tam scribe, tam tam archive, tam tam bibliothèque, quelle lec-ture faites-vous aujourd'hui? Quelle nouvelle écriture sacrée avez-vous envie de laisser à la posterité, à nos petits-enfants? Batteur, quelle nouvelle page de gloire es-tu en train d'écrire? . . . Batteur écrivain, quelle trace, quel signe es-tu en train de laisser? Tam tam au langage de l'effroi, que dites-vous? Frappez plus fort vos lettres de gloire.

(Drum scribe, drum archive, drum library, what reading are you doing today? What new sacred writing do you want to leave to posterity, to our grandchildren? Drummer, what new page of glory are you in the midst of writing? . . . Drummer-writer, what trace, what sign are you leaving? Drum with the language of fear, what are you saying? Hit your glory letters harder.) (142–43)

Similarly, Martinicans Edouard Glissant and Patrick Chamoiseau associate the drum with masculine inscription. Inserting themselves into their fictional text as a "marqueur de paroles," a "marker of words," or as it is rendered in the English translation, a "word scratcher," they literally write down what the oral artist says. While the Larousse French dictionary defines *marqueur* as a brander of animals, scorekeeper, or felt-tip pen, all of which leave graphic evidence, a *maké* has another more relevant dimension in Guadeloupean and Martinican Creole. *Maké* designates the lead drummer.

In most West African and Caribbean societies women do not play drums and are thus excluded from this particular site of inscription. What is their comparable space? How are women implicated in the general enterprise of orality? I mentioned above that studies on orality tend to neglect women's contributions, suggesting, perhaps by omission, that their roles were unimportant.[11] *Research in African Literatures* took a giant step in correcting that perception by devoting a special issue in fall 1994 to women as oral artists.

My interest was piqued on this subject when I researched an article on Senegalese women poets Annette Mbaye d'Erneville, Kiné Kirama Fall, and Ndèye Coumba Mbengue Diakhaté, mapping the ways in which they reproduce forms found in the Serer oral tradition in their French texts. I further developed my thesis about the link between women's orality and writing in an article on Mariama Bâ's *Une si longue lettre* (So Long a Letter), examining the discursive strategies that privilege the female voice. After reading traditional Bassa women's stories from Cameroon that were collected and translated into French by Werewere Liking and Marie-José Hourantier under the title *Contes d'initiation féminine du pays Bassa*, I became intrigued by how these stories for a uniquely female audience, those that articulate a "woman version," to borrow Evelyn O'Callaghan's term, can differ from the more accessible oral stories published by Birago Diop, *Les contes d'Amadou Koumba,* and Bernard Dadié, *Le pagne noir,* for example. The heroines in women's orature can be independent, intelligent, and assertive and sometimes undermine patriarchal values despite threats of punishment or censure.[12]

Francophone Women Writers of Africa and the Caribbean differs from the pioneering book-length studies on African and/or Caribbean women writers. *Ngambika: Studies of Women in African Literature,* edited by Carole Boyce Davies and Anne Adams Graves; *Out of the Kumbla: Caribbean Women and Literature,* edited by Carole Boyce Davies and Elaine Savory Fido; *Wild Women in the Whirlwind: Afra-American Culture and the Contemporary Literary Renaissance,* edited by Joanne M. Braxton and Andrée Nicola McLaughlin; and *Motherlands: Black Women's Writing from Africa, the Caribbean, and South Asia,* edited by Susheila Nasta are collections of essays by different scholars who keep separate the two geographical areas (with the exception of *Motherlands*). While these books are extremely important, they, as a whole, tend to emphasize anglophone writers. *Wild Women in the Whirlwind,* for example, devotes one chapter to the writers of Haiti, while other writers equally important from the French-speaking Caribbean are not represented at all. On the other hand, *Elles écrivent des Antilles: Haïti, Guadeloupe, Martinique* (1997), edited by Suzanne Rinne and Joëlle Vitiello, and *L'oeuvre de Maryse Condé: Questions et réponses à propos d'une écrivaine politiquement incorrecte* (1996), the proceedings of the March 1995 conference on her work offer a wide variety of critical approaches but are not yet available to the English-reading audience.

Single-author studies have become more popular recently, reflecting the growing recognition of women's literature. Irène Assiba d'Almeida's *Francophone African Women Writers: Destroying the Emptiness of Silence* (1994), Chikwenye Okonjo Ogunyemi's *Africa Wo/man Palava: The Nigerian Novel by Women* (1996), and Juliana Makuchi Nfah-Abbenyi's *Gender in African Women's Writing: Identity, Sexuality, and Difference* (1997) are excellent landmark studies that offer vigorous critical analysis grounded in the specifics of African feminism. Rangira Béatrice Gallimore's *L'oeuvre romanesque de Calixthe Beyala: Le renouveau de l'écriture féminine en Afrique francophone sub-saharienne* (1997) and Kathleen Gyssells *'Filles de Solitude': Essai sur l'identité antillaise dans les (auto)biographies de Simone et André Schwarz-Bart* (1995) are two of the few new works to center on a single francophone woman writer. Jean-Marie Volet's *La parole aux africaines ou l'idée de pouvoir chez les romancières d'expression française de l'Afrique sub-saharienne* is a broad-based study, while Odile Cazenave limits *Femmes rebelles: Naissance d'un nouveau roman africain au féminin* (1996) to francophone African women writers of the past decade. Myriam J. A. Chancy concentrates on the writers of a single country in *Framing Silence: Revolutionary Novels by Haitian Women* (1997) as does Susan Stringer in *The Senegalese Novel by Women: Through Their Own Eyes* (1996).[13]

Filomena Steady's cross-cultural perspective informs Carole Boyce Davies's *Black Women Writing and Identity: Migrations of the Subject* (1994), which considers English-speaking women's writing in Africa, the Caribbean, Black Britain, and the United States, and, on a smaller scale, Gay Wilentz's *Binding Cultures: Black Women Writers in Africa and the Diaspora*, which treats anglophone Africa and the United States.

Francophone Women Writers offers a close cross-cultural reading and analysis of selected texts by francophone writers from the African diaspora. Given the popularity worldwide of works by women from French-speaking Africa and the Caribbean, some available in English translation and a few poems and short stories accessible on the Internet, the time is right for such a critical comparative investigation. The year 1992 alone saw the English translation of Maryse Condé's *I, Tituba, Black Witch of Salem* and *Tree of Life*, both of which received a favorable assessment in the *New York Times Book Review,* and the reissue of Simone Schwarz-Bart's *Between Two Worlds.*[14] In 1996, two of Calixthe Beyala's novels appeared in translation: *Your Name Will Be Tanga* and *Loukoum: The Little Prince of Belleville;* in 1997, Mayotte Capécia's *I Am A Martinican Woman* and *The White Negress;* in 1998, Haitian Lilas Desquiron's *Reflections of Loko-Miwa;* and in 1999, Maryse Condé's *Windward Heights* (La migration des coeurs) and *Land of Many Colors* (Pays mêlé). The English translation of J. J. Dominique's *Mémoire d'une amnésique* is planned soon, and Marjolijn de Jager's translations of Werewere Liking's *Elle sera de jaspe et de corail* and *L'amour-cent-vies* will be published in one volume in the year 2000.

The first chapter of *Francophone Women Writers,* "Women and Orality," examines the ways in which African and Caribbean women are implicated in the various aspects of orality: women as singers, poets, storytellers, collectors of stories—in short, transmitters of knowledge. To further emphasize the importance of women's voice in this enterprise, borrowing Clémentine Faik-Nzuji's theories about graphic symbols in Africa and

Edouard Glissant's notion of the orality of Haitian painting, I introduce in this chapter the "oral" language of potters, wall painters, and cloth to show the ways in which women's voices are inscribed therein. I also address the ways in which women are represented in orature destined for a general public, as opposed to how they are depicted in their own stories, which will be discussed in chapter 3.

Chapter 2, "Women in Writing," examines the representation of African and Caribbean women in literature and popular culture. I discuss texts from Europe, Africa, and the Caribbean—for example, Léopold Senghor and Claire de Duras—in order to show what happens when women are objects rather than subjects, their voices not inscribed.

Chapter 3, "Appropriate(d) Orature," charts the link between women's oral and written narratives with a detailed reading of "Nguessi Ngonda," one story in Werewere Liking and Marie-José Hourantier's *Contes d'initiation féminine du pays Bassa,* and Simone Schwarz-Bart's *Pluie et vent sur Télumée Miracle* (1972). The former was originally performed during girls' initiation ceremonies in southern Cameroon and represents the authors' inscription of Bassa women's voices. The publication of the Bassa stories in French, in my opinion, marks a privileged moment in women's literature as it appropriates women's orality, inscribing and assuring its continued existence. Consequently, it will serve as a centerpiece of this study—at once a symbol of women's oral cultural heritage and an emblem of its legacy. It is also interesting to note that the issues raised in "Nguessi Ngonda" are also addressed in the other written narratives I will analyze. I argue further that Guadeloupean Simone Schwarz-Bart uses a similar strategy in *Pluie et vent sur Télumée Miracle,* in which the narrator appears to be relating her life story to an audience. Both "Nguessi Ngonda" and *Pluie et vent* are initiation tales involving the construction of identity through the intergenerational transmission of knowledge by and among women and their empowerment through cooperation.

Chapter 4, "Inscribing Friendship," is a reading of Mariama Bâ's *Une si longue lettre* (1979) and Michèle Maillet's *L'étoile noire* (1990). Although these two works were authored by a Senegalese and a Martinican, respectively, they are informed by orality and religion and they foreground women's empowerment through cooperation and inscription. The narrators, both urban middle-class women, are physically isolated, confined. Islamic custom requires that widow Ramatoulaye remain in her home for a fixed period of time, and racial and religious prejudice leads to Sidonie's imprisonment in a concentration camp during World War II. In both instances, communication is restricted and the women protagonists' voices emerge through writing. Each one keeps a diary addressed to someone else, a seeming contradiction, in which she records the pain of oppression and the role of friendship in survival.

Chapter 5, "Muffled Voices Break Free," pairs Calixthe Beyala's *C'est le soleil qui m'a brûlée* (1987) with Marie Chauvet's *Amour* (1968). Cameroon and Haiti intersect symbolically as both authors, considered controversial figures in their home countries for outspokenness, create protagonists who, marginalized by their own families as well as society, seek refuge in an interior space, finally break free, and perform an act of violent resistance. In these two narratives, women's sexuality is foregrounded, and their bodies are a site of oppression. In *Amour,* Claire keeps a diary into which she writes herself into existence, and in *C'est le soleil qui m'a brûlée,* Ateba's voice is displaced onto Moi, her spokesperson. Authors Chauvet and Beyala inscribe these voices.

Chapter 6, "Women's Life Stories as Historical Voice," is devoted to two autobiographical texts so that we may see not only the ways in which these narratives are informed by orality, but also how women's lives relate to fictional representations. Both Aoua Kéita in *Femme d'Afrique: La vie d'Aoua Kéita racontée par elle-même* (1975) and Dany Bébel-Gisler in *Léonora: L'histoire enfouie de la Guadeloupe* (1985) postulate a correspondence between their story and national history. Indeed, *histoire* in French is defined as story as well as history, in this case "herstory." *Correspondence,* with its resonances of writing, is another operative word in that Kéita chronicles the founding of the Republic of Mali. As a member of the Union Soudanaise of the Rassemblement Démocratique Africain she not only played an important role in the struggle for independence, but she inscribes women's participation as well. In a similar tradition, by translating and transcribing Léonora's story from Creole into French, Dany Bébel-Gisler permits a peasant woman to address a different audience. Léonora's text is appropriately subtitled "The Buried History of Guadeloupe," in that official records tend to ignore women's experiences. *Femme d'Afrique* and *Léonora* excavate gendered historical voices.

In all of the texts studied the writers themselves appropriate their ancestral oral tradition in which women are speaking subjects. From "Nguessi Ngonda" to *Léonora,* women's voices are meticulously inscribed. All are narrated in the first person, an affirmative "I" so to speak, a strategy designed to reproduce and privilege the female voice. Those texts in the form of a diary—*L'étoile noire*—or letters—*Une si longue lettre*— simulate a dialogue with someone else, a sort of call-and-response strategy. In that sense, they embody what Henry Louis Gates terms "speakerly texts"

(15). Precise authorship of *Contes d'initiation féminine du pays Bassa* cannot be determined. Although the collection carries the names of Were-were Liking and Marie-José Hourantier, the original authors remain anonymous. Liking and Hourantier function as recorders, transcribers, as does Dany Bébel-Gisler. In addition, these texts subvert the representation of women found in most other oral and written narratives destined for a general public, whether they be European, African, or Caribbean. These women authors, as I argue, not only inscribe women's voices, but in so doing, rewrite previous scripts, thereby conferring authority on themselves and their respective communities.

1

Women and Orality

Les contes étaient disposés en elle comme les pages d'un livre.

(The stories were ranged inside her like the pages of a book.)

Simone Schwarz-Bart, *Pluie et vent*

Cric! Crac! Ainsi commence le rituel nocturne de grand-mère.

(Cric! Crac! Thus began grandmother's nightly ritual.)

Jean-Claude Fignolé, *Les possédés de la pleine lune*

Autrefois, mes aïeules, mes semblables, veillant sur les terrasses ouvertes au ciel, se livraient aux devinettes, au hasard des proverbes, au tirage au sort des quatrains d'amour.

(In former times, my ancestors, women like myself, spending their evenings sitting on the terraces open to the sky, amused themselves with riddles or proverbs, or adding line to line to complete a love quatrain.)

Assia Djebar, *L'amour, la fantasia*

Women are heavily invested in the oral tradition of Africa and the Caribbean as producers and characters, although they are often characterized as silent.[1] In this chapter, I will discuss the ways in which they are implicated in the various aspects of orality: as singers, poets, storytellers, collectors of stories, transmitters of knowledge. To further emphasize the importance of women's voice in this enterprise, I will discuss the "oral" language of potters, wall painters, and cloth in West and Central Africa and the Caribbean. My inquiry will also include a discussion of the ways in which women are represented as characters in tales destined for a general public.

Women's voices resonate in song. Lullabies, defined as a female genre, are performed in a wide range of spaces, a single child in a small rural village to an audience of thousands in a large urban arena, as part of the repertoire of a popular singer like Angélique Kidjo from Benin.[2] Among the Lebu in Senegal there are several different categories of women's songs: *woyi njam,* songs accompanying tattooing ceremonies; *woyi tëddëte,* songs centered on love and sexuality that are performed on the occasion of the consummation of a marriage; *woyi ndëri* have love themes and are sung by young women of marriageable age; and *woyi céét* are performed by a bride's female friends and relatives as they accompany her to her new husband's home. *Woyi céét,* sung during the procession, praise the bride's lineage, encourage her to enjoy married life, advise her to stay strong despite the difficulties that lie ahead, and, finally, bid her farewell and good wishes (Ndione).

In southern Mali, Wassoulou music, which is dominated by female singers (the men's domain is dance), enjoys popularity beyond its national boundaries because vocalists such as Coumba Sidibé, Sali Sidibé, and Oumou Sangaré continue the tradition by performing as well as recording, or inscribing their voices on tapes and CDs. Sangaré, who learned her art from her mother and grandmother, pays homage to young girls in the title of her album *Ko Sira,* which translates into English as "song of the girls going to the creek." Another Malian, Kandia Kouyaté, sings praise songs as well as long tales accompanied by a kora player. Sabré Soumano, Mame Kéita, and their compatriots Les Amazones de Guinée represent their country around the world. Kéita, in particular, had to overcome the initial objections of her father when she sang in public because their family was not among the casted *griot* ones. The "go" in Les Go de Koteba translates as "cherished girl." This trio out of Côte d'Ivoire tours internationally as does Reine Pélagie, who has performed since the age of thirteen. Angélique Kidjo from Benin combines traditional Béninois, reggae, funk, samba, and Caribbean *zouk* (party) rhythms to create her own style. She recorded the voices of rural Bassila women, which she later used as backup vocalists on the song "Welcome" from the album *Fifa.* On her CD *Logozo,* she denounces the power of money in the song "Tché Tché" and the lack of public outrage concerning child poverty. One theme Tshala Muana from Zaire sings about is polygamy. As we approach the twenty-first century, compact disks and audiotapes have become important sites of the inscription of African women's voices.

In Martinique, girls used to sing traditional marriage songs (Pierre-Charles), while contemporary zouk music counts among its vocalists Chantal Djill, Edith Lefel, Joyceline Béroard, Marie-José Gibon, Tatiana Miath-Guad, Marie Céline Chrone, Corinne Denin, Josseline Varane, Lea Galva, and Nathalie Perroni, who have released albums, tapes, and CDs. Although Ina Césaire is not known as a singer, she co-wrote the songs on Malavoi's thematic album *Shè Shè,* which is centered on the memories of an old Martinican woman, Simeline. Not only do women throughout francophone Africa and the Caribbean perform the oral art of song, but many are represented on other sites of inscription. These recorded voices, which are available to unrestricted audiences, are not anonymous and can be considered the counterparts of the inscribed ones in literature.

Many scholars agree that the line separating song and poetry in Africa is an artificial one.[3] Raphaël Ndiaye's research among women poets in the village of Fadiouth, Senegal, reveals that they compose song-poems to celebrate a marriage, or a baptism, or to commemorate a family member. These poems can be sung by an individual or a group accompanied by percussion instruments. Emmanuel Matateyou notes in his article "Poésie orale traditionnelle et expression du quotidien en Afrique noire" the wide variety of themes among Bamoun women poets of Cameroon: a girl's fears at puberty, a young woman's dreams of an ideal man, complaints about mistreatment by a husband or friend, nostalgic memories of her natal village, praise for the deceased or a political party (70). The Mauritanian *tebra,* a genre of poetry composed and sung by (and to) women, has men as its subject (Voisset). Thomas Hale's work on *griottes* in Niger demonstrates their continuing and essential role during naming ceremonies, weddings, and installations of chiefs. At weddings, for example, their songs function to tease the bride, offer advice about relationships with in-laws, and invite the guests to enjoy themselves. These performers, however, are prohibited from singing about epic heroes, the province of male singers.

Poetry is only one form created and performed by female oral artists. In Mali, *tanbasire* and *worson suugu* are two gender- and class-specific narrative genres that were created by royal servants of the Jaara kingdom between the fifteenth and mid-nineteenth century. *Tanbasire* are sung by older women to an audience of their fellow servants. Mamadou Diawara collected some of these narratives from the descendants of these servant women:

> The performer always sings for one very specific person, celebrating first the history shared by the whole group of servants, then the deeds of the heroes of her own lineage and family; she does the same for the person for whom the message is intended. (Diawara 116)

Paradoxically, women are seldom celebrated in *tanbasire* (Diawara 125). While *tanbasire* celebrate the history of royal servants, *worson suugu,* accompanied by drumming, dancing, and hand clapping, poke fun at the king according to Diawara (116). Because both *tanbasire* and *worson suugu* were composed long ago, authorship cannot be assigned. Singers, therefore, are able to subvert censure and avoid punishment. What both forms have in common is that they were created and are reproduced by women of a particular class.

The dozens of essays in *La civilisation de la femme dans la tradition africaine* remind us that African women play an important role in the realms of history, the economy, politics, and art. As the guardians of culture who pass on to children values that the community cherishes, they are indispensable. Simone Schwarz-Bart summarizes the woman's place in Guadeloupean society in this way:

Ce sont les femmes qui ont tout sauvé, tout préservé, y compris l'âme des hommes. Ce sont des gardiennes jalouses qui ont toujours lutté en silence. Quand l'homme antillais faisait des enfants sans revendiquer la paternité, celle qui devait assumer la lignée, accomplir les tâches quotidiennes, s'occuper des enfants tout en leur transmettant les traditions ancestrales, c'étaient naturellement la femme.

(It is women who have saved, preserved everything, including men's souls. They are the jealous guardians who have always fought in silence. When a Caribbean man made babies without claiming paternity, the one who had to assume responsibility, accomplish the daily tasks, care for the children all while passing on to them the ancestral traditions, was naturally the woman.) (Quoted in Green 131)

Women's voices are essential in the transmission of this knowledge, especially that which pertains to girls. Trinh T. Minh-ha's assertion that "the world's earliest archives or libraries were the memories of women" (121) is relevant here in that women articulate these memories and pass them on to subsequent generations. In Mali, although practices differ slightly from community to community, the *magnamagan* is an older woman who teaches the young bride about cleanliness, hospitality, the responsibilities of being a wife. In eastern and northern Mali, instruction begins on the wedding day. On subsequent days the *magnamagan* educates the bride about the body and sexual practices. Among the Sarakolé the *magnamagan* attends the bride during the first twelve months of marriage. The activities of the *magnamagan* in Mali are essential in maintaining the equilibrium of the community. Like other crafts or professions, these practitioners train apprentices to keep certain knowledge within the group. For that reason, when Aoua Kéita, the Malian activist and midwife, asked her friend Sokona about *magnamagan's* knowledge, the information was shared with her provided she not write it down (282–83). Kéita, however, chose to inscribe this *magnamagan's* voice in her autobiography.

While the storyteller, *conteur* or *griot* is almost always figured as a male in fiction as well as studies of African and Caribbean societies, as I mentioned earlier, in Aoua Kéita's experience in Mali, mothers became storytellers when they would instruct the girls separately from the boys as part of a "traditional education." Otherwise, after dinner between the harvest and planting seasons—between November and March—the servants would narrate:

> les mères faisaient des causeries éducatives aux filles. C'est ainsi que ma mère nous narrait les contes de son lointain pays, accompagnés de douces mélodies dioula. Elle avait un thème de prédilection: ses contes portaient toujours sur les mésaventures d'une fille désobéissante qui désirant fortement le mariage d'amour, avait été malheureuse en ménage ou tuée par l'homme de son choix.

> (mothers would have educational talks with their daughters. Thus, my mother used to tell us tales, accompanied by sweet Dioula melodies, from her faraway land. She had a favorite theme; her stories always dealt with the misadventures of a disobedient girl who strongly wanting to marry for love, ended up unhappily married or killed by the man of her choice.) (16)

Women storytellers figured in other circumstances. Guadeloupean Odet Maria, in her autobiography, *Une enfance antillaise: Voyage au fond de ma mémoire,* remembers her neighbor Mademoiselle Antonia, a *grande conteuse,* whom she would visit in the evenings, and her great-aunt Fanie, whose language was rich in proverbs. Generations, gender, and geography separate Gisèle Pineau and Birago Diop; nevertheless, they both enjoyed their grandmother's tales. Pineau recalls listening to Man Ya's stories, while what Diop heard would later figure, in part, in his *Contes d'Amadou Koumba.* Calixthe Beyala is another writer who is grateful for the myths and legends told to her by her mother and grandmother (Matateyou, "Calixthe Beyala," 605–6). Ina Césaire had three different female sources of tales: her mother, Suzanne; grandmother; and servants (Schwarz-Bart, *Hommage*). Simone Schwarz-Bart pays tribute to a local storyteller Stéphanie Priccin, who died in 1968 and is the model for Télumée in *Pluie et vent sur Télumée Miracle,* with a full-page color photograph of her that closes *Hommage à la femme noire.* These women storytellers were instrumental in the transmission of knowledge—orally—to the younger generation. I wholeheartedly endorse Patrick Chamoiseau and Raphaël Confiant's concept of the *oraliturain,* a word they coin in *Lettres créoles* that captures the essence of the oral storyteller's vocation. But at the same time, I propose the use of the female equivalent, the *oralituraine,* in order to recognize women's rightful place as tellers of tales. African and Caribbean women writers are mindful to inscribe their voices.

Cloth dyeing, body decoration, and wall painting are other areas of oral expression, a form of discourse which can be considered a form of writing.[4] Among the Igbo in Nigeria, *uli* is one medium of body decoration in which one particular pattern indicates that a woman is good. In another, a woman paints vertical lines on her body when she settles an argument between her and another woman. In many parts of rural West Africa, wall painting is a communal activity involving women. Patterns and motifs, which communicate information that can vary from clan to clan, are passed from generation to generation, from mother to daughter, from expert to younger apprentice. Certain patterns are gender specific, like the calabash which represents women, while others are not. In Burkina Faso, one wall motif is a sign of longevity; another in Mauritania is a sign of welcome. Established patterns, however, do not stifle creativity. Different color combinations and methods of applying the paint (using the fingers or a spoon, for example), allow each contributor to express her own identity (Courtney-Clarke).[5]

The patterns on *pagnes* fashioned as skirts or wrappers in West and Central Africa also have their own language. It seems appropriate, then, that among the Dogon the same word is used for word and cloth (Fauque 37). Acquiring their names at the factory or in the market, *pagnes* can function in the manner of a billboard indicating the wearer's support of a political figure. Fabric printed with the image of Léopold Senghor, Sékou Touré, Thomas Sankaré, or Nelson Mandela is readily accessible. In Côte d'Ivoire twenty years ago, two patterns were associated with Madame Houphouët-Boigny, wife of the now-deceased president. After she wore one particular design, it acquired the name "diamond" and sold very well. Another cloth that appealed to customers' affection for the first lady was called the "nails of Madame Houphouët-Boigny" (Touré).

Named by wholesalers or market women to encourage sales, the messages inscribed on many of the textiles are addressed specifically to women. Some textiles are inscribed with designs that evoke proverbs and thus require intimate knowledge of the culture in order to interpret them. Among the Anyi of eastern Côte d'Ivoire, for example, one pattern suggests the proverb of "co-wife rivalry is like cow dung; the top is dry but the inside is sticky." Other textiles can express a sarcastic message, like "condolences to my husband's mistress." A pattern festooned with eyes—"my rival's eye"—indicates that the wearer is not afraid of her husband's mistress (Domowitz). A wife who wishes to convey the idea that she follows her husband who is known to go out a lot would wear a pattern with footprints named *mon pied, ton pied* (my foot, your foot) or one with a bird and cage, *si tu sors, je sors* (if you go out, I go out). *Mon mari est capable* (my husband is capable), another popular design, announces that the wearer's husband supports his family financially. I agree with Abdou Touré, who concludes that the naming of cloth has political, economic, social, and cultural implications.

In West and Central Africa, *pagne* and *page* intersect in that messages are inscribed on both surfaces, which the "reader" interprets. On the one hand, meaning is assigned by the anonymous namers of textile patterns who correspond to the unknown creators of oral stories. "Authors" of designs (those who assign names), as well as the creators of orature, remain anonymous and invisible. On the other hand, a book designates the author on its cover, forever reminding the public of its source. On each surface, however, a woman's voice is inscribed.

In Caribbean island culture, cloth is also a surface onto which meaning is inscribed. The brightly colored cotton headscarf, or *madras,* has its own language in Guadeloupe and Martinique, where traditionally a woman over eighteen would articulate her availability to suitors by the way in which she tied it. One single point indicates that she is available; with two points, she is involved with someone; three means she is married; and four indicates that she is generous to friends (Beuze 12, 20, 22). The manner of tying a *madras* can also designate a woman's profession. A vendor wears hers flat to allow a tray to sit comfortably on top of her head, while a cane cutter or coal carrier would knot hers in the back with a piece hanging down to protect her neck from the hot sun (Aumis 66).

Another form of women's oral expression that conveys meaning in Africa involves pots. In Ghana, the number of pots a woman possesses indicates status or prestige. The Fiote of Angola and the Congo practice a fascinating mode of "writing" in which pot covers are engraved with proverbs. When a woman has a grievance against her husband, she serves his meal in the pot on whose lid is inscribed the source of her complaint. She can also send a friend with whom she has quarreled a pot lid to convey certain information. In both instances, the woman avoids direct confrontation, as the pot lid serves as the intermediary (Schipper 9). All in all, the inscriptions on walls, bodies, pot covers, and cloth have the same function as the printed page; that is, women's voices conveying information.

Despite the centrality of women as producers and transmitters of culture through the oral tradition in Africa and the Caribbean, they often experience negative stereotyping as characters. Portrayed as disobedient, jealous, and incompetent, they are at times rivals for a man's attention and affection. Sociologist Fatou Sow correctly observes that portrayals of African women are either *infériorisant* (inferiorizing) or *hypervalorisant* (overvalorizing)(105), a situation which is common in orature worldwide. Mineke Schipper focuses solely on the former in her controversial collection of six hundred proverbs that stigmatize women from seventy different language groups south of the Sahara.

Woman is the source of all evil; only our soul saves us from the harm she does (Fon, Benin).

Take woman for what she is: a sister of the devil (Yoruba/Benin).

If evil is to come, it speaks through a despised woman (Ganda, Uganda).

Your wife is your favourite but also your killer (Mamprusi, Burkina Faso).

Woman's intelligence is that of a child (Benin, Senegal).

A woman and an invalid man are the same thing (Gikuyu, Kenya). (Schipper 83–89)[6]

Ama Ata Aidoo believes that Schipper's title, *Source of All Evil: African Proverbs and Sayings on Women,* and editing not only unduly stigmatize African women, but cause hurt feelings as well (167–72). The book can be read as an example of selective inscription in that it ignores proverbs complimentary to African women. A similar case can be made about the tales in Birago Diop's *Les contes d'Amadou Koumba,* originally published in 1947. The women characters, except for mothers, often embody attributes that the community deems unacceptable. It must be said that one function of proverbs and tales is pedagogical, to reinforce community values. Although the title of Diop's collection names a single source—the family griot Amadou Koumba—other people contributed stories as well: notably his brother Youssoufo, a traveling doctor; Diop himself, who traveled extensively around West Africa; and his grandmother. These are stories supplied by different ethnic groups but show similarities in their representations of women. In "N'Gor niébé" the women are gossips and cannot be trusted with a secret. In "Petit mari," disaster and death result when Koumba, coupled with her talkative daughter Khary, who usurpes her mother's role, fails to protect her son. Koumba failed the lesson this story teaches: "tant que l'enfant a sa mère, aucune peine ne peut lui être cruelle (as long as a child has a mother, it will not know great suffering) (120/20). In "N'Gor niébé" and "Petit mari," women's voices are dangerous.

One possible interpretation of "Fari l'ânesse," in that same collection, is that the female donkeys are punished for selfishness when they leave behind their famine and drought-stricken land in search of new territory. When Queen Fari and her retinue arrive in prosperous N'Guer, they decide to join the human inhabitants by transforming themselves into women. King Bour, fascinated by Fari's beauty, marries her. Eventually Fari and her courtesans become bored with their lives and ask permission to go out in the evenings, where they change back into their original form and swim and sing in the lake. One day Narr, one of the king's servants, observes the scene, memorizes the song, teaches it to the royal griot, who sings it at the court. To the horror of those present, the queen and her retinue are transformed back into donkeys and run out of town. This tale, which indicts selfishness, could also be interpreted as a woman's lack of authority over a casted individual. Not even a queen has the power to silence the servant/singer as he is about to reveal her secret.[7]

That co-wives are natural enemies is the message in "Les mamelles" (The humps). Generous, friendly, and sweet Koumba shares the information on how to get rid of her hunchback with selfish, envious, impatient, and jealous Khary. Khary does not follow directions, and as a result gains rather than loses a hump. Desperate, she throws herself into the sea. Although goodness is rewarded and evil stigmatized in this tale, there exists the underlying message of uncooperative women.

In the collection *Contes populaires du Mali* we find wicked stepmothers, rival girlfriends, and vengeful young women. The title character in "Tidian" is made to work hard by her stepmother, who relents for a time and allows Tidian to get her hair braided for a special celebration. Tidian's friends, however, trick her into taking the wrong road to the hairdresser. Lost, Tidian winds up in the serpent Balasarro's cave. He takes pity on her and braids her hair with gold and silver thread. She must agree not to reveal, however, who gave her such a beautiful hairstyle or she will die. One by one, her stepmother, father, and village chief promise her sumptuous gifts if she will tell who braided her hair. Tidian refuses until her boyfriend insists that she divulge the secret. Balasarro is so impressed by her honesty, loyalty, and discretion that he does not impose the threatened punishment. This story reproduces the idea, in addition to submission to a patriarchal figure, that a woman will be betrayed by her friends.

In "L'offense," a young woman, Diowélé, exacts revenge against her family, asking the god of the bush to punish her mother, who she feels insulted her in front of her friends. Her wish is granted and a drought ravages the country, but Diowélé escapes the suffering by seeking refuge in a tree. One by one, her mother, father, and grandfather sing to her asking for relief. Diowélé responds by asking for an even worse drought. When her boyfriend appeals to their love, she submits and asks for rain. The moral of the story—"La force de l'amour est considérable / Puisqu'elle arrive à vaincre une femme intraitable" (the power of love is considerable since it ends up conquering an inflexible woman) (88)—teaches girls the power of love.

"N'talé et N'talé sira" recalls "Les mamelles" in that it introduces rival half-sisters, one of whom is jealous. "Tléniana" involves a beautiful fairy whose marriage to a human does not last because she cannot cook. *Contes populaires du Mali,* as well as the other stories, reflect society's gender roles and teach girls about a woman's place in the community as wife and mother. Oral stories in West Africa reinforce values that are important to the entire community.

Woman as mother manages to escape negative stereotyping. She is represented as virtuous, self-sacrificing, and devoted to her husband and family. For example, Maman Caïman offers wise counsel to her children. One exception identified by Denise Paulme is "la mère dévorante" cycle in Mali, Chad, and Burkina Faso, in which a *calebasse,* a utensil associated with women, rolls uncontrollably, devouring everything in its path, including adults and children. It may appear that African women are always stigmatized in orature, which is not the case. These kinds of stories resemble more closely the ones discussed above, in which women are incompetent, disloyal, jealous, and rivals. That these tales represent women in a negative light should not lead us to conclude, like some critics, that African orature is misogynist. Because these qualities are associated with women in particular, some critics like Mohamadou Kane, Sonia Lee, and Veronika Gorog-Karady and Gérard Meyer conclude that these stories are misogynist. I disagree, preferring to consider these representations of women within their proper context.

Caribbean orature, which exists in Creole, is made accessible to other audiences largely through the efforts of women. Some collect and translate into French stories from the countryside: Emma Monplaisir, *Cric, Crac, Martinique* (1957); Arlette Bennetot, *Contes et légendes de la Guyane française* (1968); Paule de Linval, *Mon pays à travers les légendes* (1960); Joëlle Laurent and Ina Césaire, *Contes de mort et de vie aux Antilles* (1976); Ina Césaire, *Contes de nuits et de jours aux Antilles* (1989); Marie-Thérèse Julien Lung-Fou, *Contes créoles, contes animaux, proverbes, titimes ou devinettes* (1980); Sylviane Telchid, *Ti-Chika . . . et d'autres contes antillais* (1985); Mimi Barthélémy, *Malice et l'âne qui chie de l'or et autres contes d'Haïti* (1994), *Contes diaboliques d'Haïti* (1995). Suzanne

Comhaire-Sylvain published several collections of Haitian stories, among which are *Les contes haïtiens* (1938) and *Le roman de Bouqui* (1973). Women have also distinguished themselves by writing essays and critical studies on orature. Ethnologist Ina Césaire has published more than thirty articles on African and Caribbean oral traditions, and Maryse Condé's *La civilisation du bossale: Réflexions sur la littérature orale de la Guadeloupe et de la Martinique* (1978) stands as an early book-length study. Philippe Thoby-Marcelin and Pierre Marcelin single out May Humbert in their dedication to *Contes et légendes d'Haïti* (1967) for providing most of the forty-one stories.

In addition to women as collectors, researchers, scholars, and storytellers, women are characters in these Caribbean tales. How are they represented? Are they marginalized? Do they resemble their African sisters? In general, women in Caribbean stories are most often mothers, daughters, old women, witches, godmothers, stepmothers, but rarely friends or wives.

In the orature of Martinique and Guadeloupe, many stories begin with the line: "Cric? Crac! Messieurs et dames, il était une fois une mère qui avait une fille" (or "deux enfants") (Cric? Crac! Ladies and gentlemen, once upon a time there was a mother who had a daughter, [or two children]) (Laurent and Césaire). Although the mother opens most of these stories, she soon disappears. By the second or third sentence, she dies—"Un jour la mère mourut." It is as if the storyteller is compelled to connect the protagonist to a matrilineal past. Ina Césaire explains this difference between African and Caribbean stories in this way; due to the social structure in the Caribbean, the father is replaced by the mother, a situation that is reflected in the tales as well:

> au niveau de la structure sociale antillaise: le Père du conte africain disparaît—il n'apparaît d'ailleurs que tout à fait sporadiquement dans les récits antillais—et cède sa place au seul personnage qui, aux Antilles, sous-tend la cellule familiale de base: la Mère.

> (in the Caribbean social structure: the Father in the African tale disappears—he only appears sporadically in Caribbean narratives, and cedes his place to the only character who, in the Caribbean, supports the family unit, the Mother.) (78)

To illustrate her point, Césaire includes the transcription in Creole and the French translation of a Bambara story and its Guadeloupean counterpart. The Bambara begins: "Il y avait une fois un roi qui avait deux fils" (Once upon a time there was a king who had two sons) (80). On the other hand, the Guadeloupean narrative begins: "Une mère avait deux garçons" (A mother had two boys) (83). Most often the function of the mother is very limited. She is there simply to establish the matrilineal heritage of the hero. It is ironic, however, that she disappears from the tale, when in real life she remains at the center of the family.[8]

When the woman does not disappear from the text, however, the story can focus on the mother-daughter relationship. One frequent scenario is the rebellious daughter who is punished when she disobeys her wise mother. In "Tétiyette," despite her mother's warnings, young Tétiyette, who refuses all suitors, chooses a handsome stranger for a husband who ends up eating her. Luckily, her brother comes to her rescue and saves her life.[9] In another story, a girl who wants to go hunting is told by her mother that it is an activity reserved for males. Ignoring her mother's instructions, the girl catches a bird and eats it. Her stomach explodes. She is punished not only because she disobeyed her mother but because she also transgressed gender boundaries. These two stories illustrate a community ideal: girls must obey their mothers and gender roles must be strictly observed.

In Haiti, the popular Bouqui/Malice cycle rarely involves women, which is the case in the fifty tales in Suzanne Comhaire-Sylvain's *Le roman de Bouqui.* When women characters are a part of the story, they follow a familiar pattern. They disappear from the scene early on, as in "Bouqui sous le harnais," "Malice veut se marier," "Le mariage de Bouqui," because these stories are centered around Bouqui and Malice's adventures. Like their African counterparts, women are represented as negative prototypes. For example, in "Mizo" a young woman is amused by Bouqui and accepts his gifts, but does not take his proposal of marriage seriously: "Je caresse mon chien toute la journée, est-ce que j'aurais l'idée d'épouser mon chien?" (I caress my dog all day, but would I think about marrying my dog?) (25). Her greed and arrogance are punished when she approves of Mizo, a timid white stranger with an accent, who she realizes, after the marriage, is really Bouqui's dog transformed into a man temporarily for her benefit. Her attraction to (and preference for) a European man instead of a Haitian merits retaliation, according to this story. In addition, gender inferiority is inscribed by the fact that Mizo and Bouqui are named in the tale, while the woman is not. In "La mort de la famille de Bouqui," Bouqui's daughter is strangled and cut into pieces by monster Tête-sans-corps, who later eats Bouqui's wife and other children, and in "Lizette," the title character's sister Mayotte is eaten by Bouqui.

Even mothers come to a violent end in the Bouqui/Malice cycle. In "Le bain de Bouqui," Bouqui inadvertently kills his sick mother by giving her a bath in boiling water; in "Bouqui et Malice vendent leur mère," Malice tricks his partner into selling his mother in order to get money for food; and in "Ce que Malice n'a jamais pardonné à Bouqui," Malice tricks Bouqui into killing his mother so they will no longer be hungry. He convinces Bouqui to go along with this scheme:

> Nos mères sont vieilles, elles ne servent à rien et mangent toute la journée. Mangeons-les, ce sera une double économie: plus besoin de les nourrir, plus besoin d'acheter de la viande nous-mêmes. Elles doivent mourir, pas vrai? Nous devrons nous passer d'elles, nous devrons nous habituer à ne plus les revoir, à ne plus les écouter. Pourquoi attendre? Mangeons-les avant que leur chair ne soit devenue coriace.

> (Our mothers are old, they are good for nothing and eat all day. Let's eat them; it would be a double savings, no more need to feed them, no more need to buy meat. They have to die, right? We'll have to do without them, we will have to get used to not seeing them any more, to no longer listening to them. Why wait? Let's eat them before their flesh becomes tough.) (59)

However, Bouqui gets his revenge by killing and eating Malice's mother. Violence against women is common in these stories in which almost all the women are minor characters.

While female characters in the Bouqui and Malice tales are treated harshly, like many of their African counterparts, stories not a part of that cycle are not necessarily violent. One wonders if *Contes et légendes d'Haïti* provides a different perspective perhaps because the source of the tales is a woman? Philippe Thoby-Marcelin and Pierre Marcelin credit Madame May Hubert for furnishing most of the stories that make up their anthology. Women characters appear in more than half of the tales and are involved in a traditional happy ending, either marriage (as in "Jeune fille à l'étoile," in which the servant girl ends up marrying the prince) or reconciliation with loved ones (like Queen Cora, whose husband asks her forgiveness after he, suspecting that she is having an affair with one of the guards, chases her from the kingdom).

In "Maman Macaque," a lying wife is punished. Macaque transforms himself into a woman in order to marry widower Dorilas. When Dorilas learns the truth, he chases his wife from the home. On one level, the wife is punished because she lied. But there is another more subtle message. This wife did not respect her place in the home because she dominated her husband. Such behavior will not be tolerated.

Women involved in creation stories are rare in Martinique and Guadeloupe, but in Haiti a woman's anger is deemed responsible for the distance between the sky and the earth. One day, a woman, while sweeping, became annoyed by the clouds that tickled her. As she beat them with her broom, they fled higher and higher, which explains why the sky and clouds are so far away.

Woman represented as a friend is rare in the oral tradition in the Caribbean, as it is in West Africa. When there is more than one woman in a story, they are often rivals.[10] The exception seems to be "Séraphine et Lilas," best friends who get along well because they have different interests—Séraphine enjoys reading and sewing, while Lilas prefers an active social life. The depth of their friendship is illustrated when Lilas contracts leprosy and Séraphine offers to lend her her skin so that she may go dancing. Lilas, however, runs off and marries her favorite partner, leaving Séraphine behind with the unsightly skin. When Séraphine finally locates Lilas and demands her skin back, Lilas's husband, repelled by her appearance, abandons her. In addition to illustrating the importance of beauty in attracting a husband, this story also very clearly indicates that women who are friends will end up betraying each other. Whether she is found in the oral tradition of Martinique, Guadeloupe, or Haiti, the Caribbean woman follows a similar script.

African and Caribbean women are significantly implicated in orality. As producers and transmitters of, and characters in, orature, they participate in their culture's survival. In today's industrialized world, however, additional strategies are necessary. In succeeding chapters, I will examine the ways in which African and Caribbean women inscribe and thereby reclaim women's voices in their written texts.

2

Women in Writing
Representations of Women in Literature and the Media

La femme antillaise ne maîtrise pas l'image de son corps.
(The Caribbean woman does not control the image of her body.)
Ernest Pépin, "La femme antillaise et son corps"

For years, some of us have been struggling to get the world to look at the
African woman properly.
Ama Ata Aidoo, "Literature, Feminism and the African Woman Today"

African and Caribbean women have always been the object of others'
stories. Whether it was outsiders (European anthropologists, sociologists,
travel writers, novelists, poets, literary critics) or insiders (African or Caribbean *griots,* autobiographers, novelists, poets, or literary critics),
women's perspectives have been rarely presented, their voices seldom privileged. Rangira Béatrice Gallimore describes the situation, which persisted
until the 1970s, as the African woman being written neither "pour elle-
même ni par elle-même" (for herself nor by herself) (12). While women of
African descent appear as characters in literature, their voices are too often
glaringly absent. They are represented, or spoken for, their subjectivity,
their agency compromised. Christopher Miller rightfully includes Léopold
Senghor's celebrated poem "Femme noire" in this category, coining the
term *literate silence* to describe her situation (*Theories* 259).

When women began to write fiction in large numbers, however, they
created female characters who told their own stories. First-person narrators became the norm. This appropriation of voice should be seen as a
deliberate narrative strategy by writers and characters to subvert the past.
Werewere Liking and Marie-José Hourantier, for example, transcribed and
translated oral stories shared among Bassa women from Cameroon. One
of these stories, "Nguessi Ngonda," differs markedly from those told to
the general public. Before examining women's inscriptions of women's
voices, however, I will examine representations of African and Caribbean
women in literature and popular culture that has prevailed for centuries.

The portraits of African and Caribbean people in European media and literature have been shaped by the prevailing ideology. Travel writings, with their dichotomy of the positive Self and negative Other, mirrored colonial discourse; they both created myths and stereotypes that served the colonial enterprise. Scientific studies on skull size also purported that Africans were physically closer to animals and thus intellectually inferior to whites. As a result, blacks were represented as cannibals—savage, primitive, nonhuman.[1] In his *Cahier d'un retour au pays natal,* Aimé Césaire protests these constructions:

> Et ce pays cria pendant des siècles que nous sommes des bêtes brutes; que les pulsations de l'humanité s'arrêtent aux portes de la négrerie; que nous sommes un fumier ambulant hideusement prometteur de cannes tendres et de coton soyeux.

> (For centuries this country repeated that we are brute beasts; that the human heart-beat stops at the gates of the black world; that we are walking manure hideously proffering the promise of tender cane and silky cotton.) (38/67)

Joseph Zobel's young narrator in *La rue cases-nègres* likewise complains that the black characters he sees in feature films have no basis in reality:

> qui a créé pour le cinéma et le théâtre ce type de nègre, boy, chauffeur, valet de pied, truand, prétexte à mots d'esprit faciles, toujours roulant des yeux blancs de stupeur, affichant un inextinguible sourire niais, générateur de moquerie? Ce nègre d'un comportement grotesque sous le coup de botte au cul que lui administre fièrement le Blanc, ou lorsque ce dernier l'a eu berné avec la facilité qui s'explique par la théorie du "nègre-grand-enfant"?
>
> Qui a inventé pour les nègres qu'on montre au cinéma et au théâtre ce langage que les nègres n'ont jamais su parler, et dans lequel, je suis certain, aucun nègre ne réussirait à s'exprimer? Qui a, pour le nègre, convenu une fois pour toutes de ces costumes à carreaux qu'aucun nègre n'a jamais fabriqués ou portés de son choix?

> (who was it who created for the cinema and the theater that type of black man, houseboy, driver, footman, truant, a pretext for words from simple minds, always rolling their white eyes in amazement, always with a silly irrepressible smile plastered on their faces, provoker of mockery? That black man with his grotesque behavior under the kick in his backside proudly administered by the white man,

or when the latter had him hoodwinked with an ease that is explained by the theory of the "black man being a big child"?

Who was it who invented for the blacks portrayed in the cinema and in the theater that language the blacks never could speak and in which, I am sure, no black man will manage to express himself? Who was it who, for the black man, agreed once and for all, on those plaid suits that no black man ever made or wore of his own choice?) (289/ 168–69)

It becomes the task of the writer, then, to deconstruct these powerful visual images. As Edouard Glissant asserts so persuasively in *Le discours antillais,* it is necessary to develop a poetics of the subject: "pour cela même qu'on nous a trop longtemps 'objectivés' ou plutôt 'objectés'" (if only because we have been too long "objectified" or rather "objected to") (257/149).

Absent from these observations, however, is a condemnation of the ways in which black women's bodies are exploited, the ways in which their voices are not inscribed. Sander Gilman has shown that in the West, black women's bodies are associated with pathology.[2] V. Y. Mudimbe in *The Invention of Africa* cites a 1700 Andreas Schulter painting titled "Africa," which depicts a nude woman behind whom stands a lion as an example of the association between animals and African women (12). To these representations can be added the South African Sara Bartman, renamed the Hottentot Venus, whose large buttocks attracted spectators to European sideshows in the early nineteenth century. During the 1920s and 1930s, Josephine Baker's body was on public display in Europe in a not too dissimilar manner. Her tremendous success was brought on by her trademark, dancing bare breasted in a banana skirt with a jungle background, and her appearances in films—*Princesse Tam Tam* (1935) and *Zouzou* (1934)—in which she played the role of a "primitive" brought to France to be "civilized." The male European voyeuristic gaze inscribed its own fantasies on her naked body, as illustrated in the opening sentences of Jean-Claude Baker's biography *Josephine Baker: The Hungry Heart:*

> "Quel cul elle a!" What an ass! Excuse the expression, but that is the cry that greeted Josephine as she exploded onstage in "La Danse de Sauvage." (Sixty years later, her friend and sometimes lover, Maurice Bataille, would say to me, "Ah! ce cul . . . it gave all of Paris a hard-on.") (3)

According to Jean-Claude Baker, naked female body parts were used to attract audiences to "La revue nègre": "We need tits. These French people, with their fantasies of black girls, we must give them 'des nichons'" (111). Sexuality, animality, and derision converge in the visual representation of Josephine Baker as evidenced by this comment attributed to André Levinson: "the splendor of an ancient animal, until the movements of her behind and her grin of a benevolent cannibal make admiring spectators laugh" (7). In many photographs, posters, lithographs, sculptures, sketches, and drawings she is shown crouched in the manner of or next to a predatory animal or caricatured with large lips, breasts, and rear end.[3] Reviewers used words like savage, exotic, comic, and childlike to describe her. Initially, Baker had little control over how she was represented. As she reveals in her memoirs, she was nervous and reluctant about posing completely nude for the publicity poster for "La revue nègre." Artist Paul Colin insisted to the point where he removed her underwear. Gradually, Baker admits in her autobiography, *Josephine,* that she became more relaxed and accepted the situation (50). She eventually became an accomplice in the representation of herself by appearing in public with her snake or cheetah. The Baker phenomenon not only reflected but reinforced stereotypes about black women.

Caricatures of African and Caribbean women with oversized lips, cheeks, breasts, and earrings were also prevalent in French advertising.[4] As late as the mid-1980s, I recall seeing a billboard in Paris showing a naked black woman on whose exaggerated backside sat an uncorked bottle of wine (or champagne) releasing its contents to a waiting glass, an obvious updating of the Hottentot Venus image. This is an illustration of what bell hooks contends in *Black Looks: Race and Representation* is the heightened sexuality attributed to black women (63).

These kinds of representations show no signs of abating. One Folio edition of *Moi, Tituba sorcière,* to Maryse Condé's consternation, reproduces Benoist's "Portrait de négresse," a painting currently hanging in the Louvre, showing an African woman seated with her right breast exposed, which has nothing at all to do with the novel's plot.[5] The cover of Pierre Pluchon's *Vaudou, sorciers, empoisonneurs de Saint-Domingue à Haïti* (1987) (Voodoo, witches, poisoners from Saint Domingue to Haiti) pictures a grimacing Haitian woman with eyes closed, biting a long saber.

On the other hand, in the French *imaginaire,* the closer a black woman's phenotype resembles that of a white woman, the more she is considered beautiful and worthy of promoting French consumer products. Voluptuous, barefoot, smiling, and wearing a headscarf *(madras)* and earrings, that Caribbean woman was featured on French posters and packaging for rum and toothpaste.[6] Also, marketers exploit Caribbean woman's bodies when they use them alongside pristine beaches and blue skies in print campaigns and television commercials to attract tourists to the islands. Again, the black woman's sexuality and status as a commodity are accentuated.

The way in which the Creole punch "Tropic" is marketed makes a particular statement about racial and gender power relations as well. The print advertising for the product shows a black servant, a model of submission, gazing adoringly at her white mistress while holding a parasol over her head,[7] an image that was reproduced in the New York Times during President Clinton's visit to Uganda in 1998. Janet Museveni, the first lady, is pictured seated, holding a parasol over Clinton's head. What appears to some as a gesture of hospitality can also be read as a throwback to familiar colonial photographs of black domestics and their employers. What all of these visual representations have in common is a particular discourse that constructs an object of consumption—"consumption by looking, as well as often quite literally by purchase," says Annette Kuhn in The Power of the Image (19). Taken as a whole, these representations illustrate myths and fantasies about animality, sexuality, and servility, what bell hooks calls "consumer cannibalism" (Black Looks 31).[8]

Numerous full-length studies document a similar stereotyping in French literature,[9] therefore I will confine my remarks to Ourika, a novel by Claire de Duras, an antislavery activist who nonetheless reproduces colonial discourse. The cover of the 1826 edition of the novel shows Senegalese Ourika, rescued from slavery as a child and brought to France, seated, dressed in a nun's white habit, gazing up at a white male who is standing.[10] He is the doctor who comes to the convent to treat her (and is surprised that she is articulate and polite), but his primary function in the text is to introduce, relate, and frame Ourika's story, thereby lending credibility and legitimizing her narrative. The message is that she alone does not have that authority because of her race and sex.

Claire de Duras's character Ourika internalizes the racist perceptions prevalent about black people during the nineteenth century. At the age of fifteen, she overhears her benefactor, Madame de B, who sheltered her from the outside world, discussing her limited future because of her race. That moment marks a change in Ourika's life. From then on, she associates her dark skin with dependency, scorn, poverty, and loneliness. Noticing her hands: "je croyais voir celles d'un singe; je m'exagérais ma laideur, et cette couleur me paraissait comme le signe de ma réprobation" (I thought I saw [the hands] of a monkey; I exaggerated my ugliness and this color seemed to me like the sign of my reprobation) (15). She is haunted by her physical appearance, "cette physionomie dédaigneuse" (this disdainful physiognomy) (28), and takes steps to render herself invisible; she removes all mirrors from her room and wears clothes that completely cover her body. She laments "J'aurais voulu être transportée dans ma patrie barbare, au milieu des sauvages qui l'habitent" (I would have wanted to be transported back to my barbarous country, amidst the savages who live there) (28). Shame characterizes her reaction to the killing of whites during the Haitian revolution. She distances herself from those responsible, calling them "race de barbares et d'assassins" (a race of barbarians and assassins) (20). Ourika, the victim of prejudice herself, is a character consumed by self-hate and alienation who embraces the ideal of white womanhood, a condition later discussed by Frantz Fanon in *Peau noire, masques blancs* (Black Skin, White Masks). The public sympathized with Ourika to the point that she was celebrated in poems and paintings.[11]

All of these representations of black women articulate their distance from the Western ideal of physical beauty, what it considers the idealized center of harmony, symmetry, and equilibrium. The black woman's "otherness" from white women is located far beyond mere difference. Western female beauty is figured in blondness, purity, fragility, thin lips, and a small rear end.[12] The black woman is eroticized, rendered grotesque, and objectified in literature and popular culture. What Ernest Pépin correctly posits about Caribbean women—that they do not control the image of their own bodies, which are represented as "corps aliéné, corps marchandise, corps souffrant" (alienated body, commodity body, suffering body), is equally true for African women ("La femme antillaise" 193). Racism and sexism inform their representation.

In African literature, as in orature, mothers are celebrated and glorified as the personification of Africa. Léopold Sédar Senghor's "Femme noire," published in *Chants d'ombre* (1945), is the most well-known example. In the poem's first stanza the adult narrator recalls his mother's role as a protector: "J'ai grandi à ton ombre, la douceur de tes mains bandait mes yeux" (I grew up in your shadow. The softness of your hands shielded my eyes) (270/8). Camara Laye followed Senghor's model in the dedication to *L'enfant noir* (1953). In the form of a prose poem, it reads:

Femme noire, femme africaine, ô toi ma mère je pense à toi . . . O Dâman, ô ma mère, toi qui me portas sur le dos, toi qui m'allaitas, toi qui gouvernas mes premiers pas, toi qui la première m'ouvris les yeux aux prodiges de la terre, je pense à toi.

(Black woman, African woman, Oh, my mother I think of you . . . O my mother, you who carried me on your back, you who nursed me,

you who guided my first steps, you who first opened my eyes to the
wonders of the earth, I think of you.)

The mother in this autobiographical narrative is extremely devoted and
protective of her son, like the mothers found in orature. Both Senghor and
Camara Laye, far away from home, associated the body of *mère* (mother)
with *terre* (Africa). The female body—the hands, specifically—protected
Senghor from the sun;[13] Camara Laye recalls her back, breasts, and hands.
The sons' longing for the absent mother metaphorically represents their
nostalgia for Africa. This view from afar—both geographical and tempo-
ral—caused the writers to idealize their *mère/terre,* one characteristic of
negritude. Senegalese poet Lamine Diakhaté states explicitly that he celebrates Africa through her women in his two collections *La joie d'un continent* (1955) and *Le temps des mémoires* (1967): "Je chante l'Afrique à
travers la femme. Elle est source d'inspiration dans ces diverses fonctions
et symbolise le continent" (I sing Africa through women. They are the
source of inspiration in their diverse functions and symbolize the continent).[14] Poet David Diop associates his mother and a black woman dancer
with Africa in "A ma mère" and "A une danseuse noire." The struggles
of motherhood, including pregnancy and childbirth, however, are passed
over. These writers also overcompensated for the stereotypical images of
women (read: Africa) discussed above that were prevalent at the time.

That Senghor, Laye, Diakhaté, and Diop associated women/mothers
with their native continent was understandable, because according to sociologist Fatou Sow: "La terre, porteuse de vie, est symbolisée de manière
variée selon les ethnies et les terroirs, mais elle est partout symbole de
féminité (The earth, giver of life, is symbolized in various ways by ethnic
groups and areas, but it is a symbol of femininity everywhere) (107). In
addition, in African societies not only is motherhood an expectation, it is
a privileged role. According to Ifi Amadiume in *Male Daughters, Female
Husbands,* "maternity is viewed as sacred in the traditions of all African
societies. And in all of them, the earth's fertility is traditionally linked to
women's maternal powers. Hence the centrality of women as producers
and providers and the reverence in which they are held" (191). Consequently, male writers idealize their mothers in their works.[15] Perhaps
Ousmane Sembène sums it up best in the closing of his short story in
Voltaïque titled "La mère" (The mother): "L'immensité des océans n'est
rien à côté de l'immensité de la tendresse d'une mère" (the boundless ocean
is nothing compared to the boundless tenderness of a mother)(42/39).

With the advent of independence and autocratic neocolonial regimes, some male writers constructed their women characters as Africa, but in a different way. No longer symbolic of a glorious past like Senghor's "Femme noire," their bodies can represent the new nation violated by its own people. Salimata, in Ahmadou Kourouma's *Les soleils des indépendances* (The suns of independence) (1968), is battered and raped. Ashamed and ostracized by the community because she cannot become pregnant, she has "le destin d'une femme stérile comme l'harmattan et la cendre" (her destiny is not fertile like the soil, but rather like the dry African wind and ashes that do not produce anything) (30). Ironically, it is revealed later that it is Fama who is in fact sterile. That Salimata was raped by Tiécoura, a *féticheur,* and robbed by the beggars she was trying to help feed symbolizes not only the violation of trust between men and women, between the powerful and the powerless, but also the pillage of Africa by one of her own.

Mongo Beti is another writer who subverts the mère/terre trope. In the dedication to *Remember Ruben* (1974), he explicitly makes the connection between mother and motherland: "To Diop Blondin, proud son of Africa, my young brother, murdered in the foul prisons of an African ruler. *Africa, harsh mother, forever fertile in mercenary tyrants!*" (emphasis added). The eponymous heroine of his *Perpétue* (1974) is another good example. Forced by her mother to quit school and marry Edouard so the family can obtain the dowry, Perpétue is then subjected to several beatings and forced by her husband to have an affair with M'Barg Onana, a man who could advance his career. Perpétue's life as a victim of exploitation and oppression mirrors the situation in Cameroon under a corrupt neocolonial government. It is significant, too, that Perpétue does not narrate her own story.

Although Ferdinand Oyono's *Le vieux nègre et la médaille* (The Old Man and the Medal) was published in 1956, prior to the establishment of independent nations, Kelara can still be put in this category. Childless because her two sons died fighting for France in the war, she and her husband represent the collaboration between colonized (Africa) and colonizer (Europe). The result is the destruction of the family through the loss of sons who leave no offspring. More important, perhaps, is the fact that Kelara is, at one point in the novel, rendered speechless.

In between the representation of woman as the romanticized African past or the corrupt present one can situate La Grande Royale of Cheikh Hamidou Kane's *L'aventure ambiguë* (Ambiguous Adventure)(1962). Almost six feet tall and sixty years old, she is physically imposing. Older sister of the chief, she is highly respected by all as a keeper of tradition, yet she is the instigator of change. It is she who for the first time invites the women to a meeting of the Diallobé clan to discuss an important decision. There she announces her recommendation that they send their children to the French school, even though she dislikes what it represents. The narrator comments:

> Il (Samba Diallo) avait souvent vu la Grande Royale se dresser, seule, contre l'ensemble des hommes de la famille Diallobé, groupés autour du maître. Sur le moment, elle était toujours victorieuse, parce que nul n'osait lui tenir tête longtemps. Elle était l'aînée.

> (He had often seen the Most Royal Lady stand up alone, against the men of the Diallobé family. At the moment she was always victorious, because no one dared hold out against her for long. She was the first born.) (49/32)

What distinguishes La Grande Royale from most other women characters is that she is neither a wife or a mother. Not only does she speak in public, but people listen because of her aristocratic-class status. La Grande Royale contrasts markedly to women in some other African ethnic groups. According to Aoua Kéita, up until the 1950s Sarakolé, Peul, Moorish, and Bambara women could not attend meetings with men and

> parler en public à haute voix était sacrilège pour une femme de bonne famille. Même dans un groupement de femmes, elles se servaient toujours de femmes ou d'hommes de caste qui communiquaient leurs pensées à l'assemblée.

> (speaking in public was sacrilegious for a woman from a good family. Even in a group, they always used casted men or women who communicated their thoughts to the group.) (297–98)

Consequently, many wives are represented in African fiction as being passive and silent. A writer such as Ousmane Sembène, who is acclaimed for creating a variety of female characters, ironically, sums up a traditional women's destiny as being one of submission, docility, and modesty. Assitan in *Les bouts de bois de Dieu* (God's Bits of Wood) embodies such a wife:

> Assitan était une épouse parfaite selon les anciennes traditions africaines: docile, soumise, travailleuse, elle ne disait jamais un mot plus haut que l'autre . . . Son lot à elle, son lot de femme était d'accepter et de se taire, ainsi qu'on le lui avait enseigné.

> (By the ancient standards of Africa, Assitan was a perfect wife: docile, submissive, and hard-working, she never spoke one word louder

than another . . . Her own lot as a woman was to accept things as they were and to remain silent, as she had been taught to do.) (170–71/ 148–49)

But when a woman does not follow the prescribed order—that is, marry the person chosen by her parents and have children, she is often represented as a prostitute in African literature. Ngon-Minlan in Martin Enobo-Kosso's *Monologue d'une veuve angoissée,* Ebela in Omo Ya Eku's *La prison sous le slip d'Ebela,* and Seynabou Diagne in Mamadou Samb's *De pulpe et d'orange: Autobiographie d'une prostituée dans une ville africaine,* all lead self-destructive lives as victims of society.[16] Fatou Zalme signs Patrick G. Ilboudo's *Les carnets secrets d'une fille de joie.* Ya in V. Y. Mudimbe's *Le bel immonde* (Before the Birth of the Moon) chooses the life of a bar girl to avoid the stifling life of a traditional wife: "C'est la routine qui m'a fait fuir: les enfants, la cuisine, les champs, les puits à longueur d'années (It was the predictable routine that made me flee: children, cooking, field work, the well, until the end of my days) (99/122). Gender divisions limit women's choices. As she had been told by a schoolteacher:

Pour les hommes, il y avait les chantiers; pour les meilleurs d'entre eux, des écoles de médecine ou d'agronomie. Pour une femme, pour toi, il n'avait que le mariage, seul possible dans une absence totale d'avenir.

(For the men there were construction sites; for the best among them there were medical schools or schools of agronomics. For a woman, for you, there was only marriage, the only possibility in what was a completely nonexistent future.) (56/71)

On the other hand, Penda in Sembène's *Les bouts de bois de Dieu,* called a whore by her neighbors because of her "periodic escapades" (190), evolves during the course of the story to the point where she speaks for herself and the other women. She becomes involved in the railway workers' strike, first by supervising the distribution of rations to women, then by leading a band of children to steal rice from the Syrian merchant. She eventually becomes a committed strike member, assuming a leadership position among the women and becoming their spokesperson: "Je parle au nom de toutes les femmes, mais je ne suis que leur porte-parole. Pour nous cette grève, c'est la possibilité d'une vie meilleure . . . Et demain nous allons marcher jusqu'à N'Dakarou" (I speak in the name of all the women, but I am just the voice they have chosen to tell you what they have decided to do . . . For us women this strike means the possibility of a better life tomorrow.

So we have decided that tomorrow we will march together to Dakar) (288/254). It is the first time in memory that a woman has spoken in public in Thiès. Mindful of the husbands' presence in the crowd, however, she retreats slightly by asking for their permission: "Hommes, laissez vos épouses venir avec nous!" (Men, you must allow your wives to come with us!) (289/255).

Sembène not only offers a sympathetic portrait of a prostitute who becomes a spokesperson for the women and then martyr for the entire group, he also implies that prostitution knows no gender. At one point in the narrative Bakayoko suggests that some males like himself are forced to work for the French, while others prostitute themselves morally.

Young women educated in the French school and who become alienated from their community are constructed similarly. Ndèye Touti, an assimilationist to the core in Ousmane Sembène's *Les bouts de bois de Dieu*, is blinded by the promises of French culture. Although she never attended French school, Diouna of Sembène's "La noire de . . ." is another such character. Leaving Senegal to move to the south of France with her employers, she thinks life will be full of opportunity. Once in France, however, she is exploited and shown off by her employers as an exotic object. Feeling isolated and cut off from all ties to her homeland, she commits suicide. Abdoulaye Sadji offers another perspective of this kind of character in *Maïmouna, petite fille noire* (1953). The protagonist, a young village girl, joins her married sister Rihanna in Dakar, where she finds an unfamiliar life with many problems. The novel's straightforward message about remaining at home and avoiding the big city makes it resemble an oral story. Sadji's *Nini, mulâtresse du Sénégal* (1954, 1965) is a similar story of alienation. Nini, of mixed race from Saint-Louis, is prejudiced against blacks and wants to marry a white man. Her choice is Martineau, who abandons her to marry a Frenchwoman. Nini had, after all, only followed in the footsteps of her aunt Hortense and grandmother Hélène. What is interesting, though, is that these two older women later try to correct their past mistakes by attempting to reintegrate themselves into their formerly rejected community.

Women educated in the French school are not always alienated from their community. To highlight this position, this kind of character is balanced with an older woman character who is tied to tradition. One such character is Rama, the daughter in *Xala*, who tries to convince her mother, Adja Awa Astou, to leave her polygamous husband, El Hadji Abdou Kader Bèye.

On the other hand, when women collectively rebel against oppression, there is another outcome. In Mongo Beti's *La ruine presque cocasse d'un polichinelle* (Lament for an African Pol) (1979), the women of Ekoumdoum mobilize and force the corrupt government to obtain medicine for their dying children. This effort is only one of many that brings about change in the community. In Francis Bebey's *La poupée ashanti* (1973), market women demonstrate in support of Madame Amiofi when she loses her vendor's license because her husband is a member of the opposition. In Ousmane Sembène's *Les bouts de bois de Dieu* (God's Bits of Wood), the women battle the French police and organize a march from Thiès to Dakar in support of the striking railway workers. While the point is made that solidarity leads to success, some gender issues are not addressed; as the narrative closes, the women return to their domestic chores.[17]

We can draw certain conclusions about women characters in texts by African men. Rarely are they the protagonists. Even when the title carries a woman's name, she is not necessarily at the center of the text, nor is her voice privileged. *Perpétue* names the heroine, but she is dead when the novel opens. It is her older brother Essola who reconstructs her life as he investigates the reasons for her death.[18] The text is actually his story and not hers. The same can be said of Joseph-Jules Mokto's *Ramitou, mon étrangère* (1971), Pierre Makombo Bamboté's *Princesse Mandapu* (1972), Marouba Fall's *La collégienne* (1990), and Cheik Aliou Ndao's *Excellence, vos épouses!* (1983), where it is not a question of the woman's story. On the other hand, the second part of Joseph Owono's *Tante Bella* (1959) is actually her story, read aloud by one of the characters—a French pharmacist—to the gathered guests. Tante Bella's voice, however, is mediated by that of a white male, and thus marginalized like Ourika's. On the other hand, women's voices frame *Les bouts de bois de Dieu;* the first chapter, titled "Adjibidji," opens in a courtyard in Bamako as a group of women talk. The narrative closes on blind Maïmouna's song.[19]

Often when there are important women characters in texts created by African men, there is a similar script. Victim or militant, the woman dies—either she is killed or commits suicide: prostitute Ebela is beaten to death; Perpétue dies in her sleep; princess Doguicimi buries herself alive alongside her husband's body; Penda is shot leading the women's march; Princesse Mandapu is burned by an overturned pot of boiling water; Raki and her child die during childbirth in Cheik Aliou Ndao's *Buur tilleen, roi de la Médina;* Monique drowns in Amadou Koné's *Les frasques d'Ebinto* (1975). Diouna in "La noire de . . ."; Ngoné War Thiandum, mother of incest victim in *Véhi ciosane;* Ouly Thiam in Marouba Fall's *La collégienne;* and Yavelde in Sony Labou Tansi's *L'anté-peuple* all commit suicide. If the woman does not die, however, another possible outcome is a happy marriage: Marième marries Karim in Ousmane Socé's *Karim* (1935); Kany and Samou in Seydou Badian's *Sous l'orage* (1963); Ramitou and Jules in Joseph-Jules Mokto's *Ramitou, mon étrangère* (1971); Edna and Spio in Francis Bebey's *La poupée ashanti* (1973); Wazzi and Assamoa in Jean Dodo's *Wazzi* (1977).

The Congolese writer Henri Lopès rewrites the script in *La nouvelle romance* (1976). Wali accompanies her husband Bienvenu N'Kama, a former soccer player, to Brussels when he is named to a diplomatic post for which he is not qualified. There she resumes her formal education, which she had abandoned earlier to care for the children of Bienvenu's sister. The new experience in Europe coupled with her experiences and discussions with friends at home broaden Wali's perspective. More conscious of the limited possibilities of the submissive wife preferred by her husband, she chooses to stay in Europe when he is called home. *La nouvelle romance* offers a new and different representation of women. Not only is Wali at the center, it is indeed her story. Second, she is not seen as inadequate like Salimata in *Les soleils des indépendances* because she has not given birth. Third, the reader sees her interact successfully with friends Awa and Elise, a rarity in most oral or written texts. Fourth, Wali's stay in the West does not lead to her alienation. Her objective to learn more is no selfish goal; she plans to use her new knowledge to change gender inequities in the Congo on her return.[20] Lopès's *Sur l'autre rive* takes women one step further in that it is narrated in the first person by a woman, Marie-Eve. However, in his most recent novel, *Le lys et le flamboyant,* the protagonist, Simone Fragonard, or Monette, does not speak for herself, but her story is narrated by her male cousin.

In francophone Caribbean literature by male writers, the woman is often confined to the margins. In Martinique and Guadeloupe, she is not associated with the white sandy beaches as she is in Western popular culture (in these texts the sea is inaccessible; it separates the city from the countryside, the past from the future), but with the stifling cane fields or plantation kitchens, what Edouard Glissant would consider "alienating landscapes."[21] One such woman, a peasant who stands and urinates, is seen in Aimé Césaire's *Cahier.* As discussed earlier, in the orature of Martinique and Guadeloupe, women are represented as mother figures; however, Césaire does not romanticize his mother in the *Cahier,* recalling her pedaling the Singer sewing machine night and day to earn money to feed the family.

Other mothers in Caribbean literature are similarly represented, but almost always without a husband. In Joseph Zobel's *La rue cases-nègres*, which takes place in Martinique of the 1930s, there is a variety of single rural women who surround young protagonist José Hassam. Délia, José's mother, is alone after Eugène, José's father, is killed in the war; Madame Amélius, José's godmother, is a widow whose daughter and brother are also dead; Madame Léonce, who takes advantage of José by making him work for his lunch, has a husband who never appears in the text. Mam'zelle Gracieuse, Jojo's mother, is deserted by Justin Roc when he marries someone else (Justin Roc himself was fathered by the plantation owner and one of his workers—one can assume that Justin's father did not marry his mother). M'man Tine—Amantine—never married after she was raped by her employer. She raises grandson José alone in order to allow her daughter Délia to enjoy a better life as a domestic worker in the city. M'man Tine is hard working and self-sacrificing.

When M'man Tine is first introduced, it is sundown and she is returning exhausted from the cane fields, her dress torn, her feet hardened and swollen, but she has saved part of her meager lunch as a treat for José. Later on, when she is forced to bring him with her to the cane fields, she shields him from the hot sun with her shadow (which echoes Senghor's recollection of his mother's shadow sheltering him from the sun). *La rue cases-nègres* closes as M'man Tine dies and José recollects her gnarled hands, whose work permitted him to attend school.[22] According to José these signs of hard work and self-sacrifice are typical of older poor black mothers.

> Et bien! C'est à croire que vraiment cette catégorie de femmes que sont les vieilles mères noires et pauvres détiennent, dans le coeur qui bat sous leurs haillons, comme un pouvoir de changer la crasse en or, de rêver et de vouloir avec une telle ferveur que, de leurs mains terreuses, suantes et vides, peuvent éclore les réalités les plus palpables, les plus immaculées et les plus précieuses.

> (Well! It really looked as if that category of women as represented by the old black, unfortunate mothers did possess in their hearts, beating under their rags, some sort of power to change dirt into gold, to dream and to wish for something so ardently that, from their earth-stained sweating, empty hands, could appear the most palpable, the most immaculate and the most precious of realities.) (185/107)

Such women suffer loss and sometimes violence, but they are proud and dignified and persevere despite tremendous odds. Gender boundaries are transgressed, as they are not only the caretakers of children but the principal family breadwinners as well. We have already seen how despite her age, M'man Tine endures back-breaking hours in the cane fields so that José will not have to. Later, Délia takes in laundry to pay for José's school fees in Fort-de-France. In addition, it is M'man Tine who teaches her grandson to fish. While it is significant that the narrator singles out mothers for praise, he does not in any way romanticize their struggle.[23]

While there are different social classes of women in *La rue cases-nègres*, Zobel does not privilege light-skinned women over their dark-skinned sisters as we saw in European popular culture. Prejudice and alienation can occur in any group. Jojo's stepmother, M'man Yaya, is cruel. Although her maid, M'mzelle Mélie, is a member of the same social class as José, she denounces his culture and his language (even though she speaks only Creole). Brown-skinned Adréa, the cashier in the bar friends José, Jojo, and Carmen frequent in Fort-de-France, denounces the entire race and cannot understand why her light-skinned mother deigned to sleep with a black man.[24] On the other hand, while José is fascinated by his light-skinned female elementary school teachers, he realizes that they are the agents of a biased French curriculum.

Writers like Edouard Glissant and Patrick Chamoiseau do not generally place women at the center of their narratives. Glissant's novels, which at times feature the same characters, present Marie Celat, Mycéa, whose story takes precedence only in *La case du commandeur*. Although Marie-Sophie Laborieux is the principal narrator in Chamoiseau's *Texaco*, the story she tells is not solely her own, but rather her father's, and centers on the establishment of the urban community.

Haitian literature, which has a longer history than that of Martinique and Guadeloupe, provides a better barometer of the representation of female characters. Several studies have considered the representation of women characters by male writers.[25] Léon-François Hoffmann makes several important points on the subject that deserve mention here. Male writers celebrate the beauty of light-skinned women, but not that of their dark-skinned counterparts. They are associated positively with the nation, like we saw above in certain African poets. Unlike them, however, when the woman's body is evoked, it is not the body of the mother that we saw in Léopold Senghor[26] and Camara Laye, but rather the body of a potential lover whose sexuality is accentuated. Hoffmann cites examples from Emile Roumer, Carl Brouard, Luc Grimard, Lorimer Denis, and Oswald Durand, all of whom identify women with appetizing fruit: "le corps de l'Haïtienne est vu comme une véritable corbeille de fruits tropicaux (the Haitian woman's body is seen like a real bowl of tropical fruit) ("L'image" 197).

Joan Dayan sees a similar objectification of women in René Dépestre's collection of short stories *Alléluia pour une femme-jardin* in which the admiring male gazes upon the female. This idealization, however, also brings disempowerment as the evocation of her body parts reveals a desire for "ravishment and mutilation" ("Hallelujah" 585).[27]

Dépestre's poem "Bref éloge de la langue française" has silent women as its center. As the poem opens, the narrator states that now and again it is a good idea to bring the French language to the river and rub its body with perfumed herbs—that is, Creole words. This metaphor suggests the work of a laundress who traditionally does the washing in the river. The poem closes on another woman who happily unties her skirt to be caressed, fondled by the poet:

> oui je chante la langue française
> qui défait joyeusement sa jupe
> ses cheveux et son aventure
> sous mes mains amoureuses de potier.

> (yes I sing the French language
> who joyously unties her skirt
> her hair and her adventure
> under my loving potter's hands.) (33)

Thus, Dépestre compares the enrichment of the French language with the infusion, inclusion of Creole expressions with making love to a receptive woman. This eroticized female appears often in Haitian literature.

Jacques Roumain's women are not a collection of body parts, but whole women. The female elite in *Les fantoches* are frivolous and not concerned with the reality of the American occupation of their country. *Gouverneurs de la rosée* provides yet another interesting perspective. Peasant Délira mourns her miserable condition and waits for death as the novel opens. She is passive and resigned to her fate as drought overtakes the countryside. With the return of her son Manuel, however, she begins to change. When he is killed, she takes his place as an intermediary and reconciles the two enemy camps, a role that is often overlooked by critics. Unity and solidarity will solve the village's problems, and Délira is partly responsible for that happening. Manuel, whose mission is inscribed in his name— Emmanuel, "élu," the chosen one who brings *eau* (water)—is complemented by his mother, Délira Délivrance, who "delivers" Fonds-Rouge from its dilemma.[28] Annaïse, Manuel's girlfriend, also has a role in convincing her relatives to listen to reason. Although she resembles more closely the voluptuous peasant type, her body does not have the same purpose as in Dépestre's text.

Jacques-Stéphen Alexis has been applauded for his enlightened attitude toward women in his novels. Many are independent and even resist male violence: Joyeuse Pitou and Léonie of *Les arbres musiciens* and Consuelo Morales in *Compère Général Soleil,* for example.[29] However, when Claire-Heureuse in *Compère* is slapped by her husband, Hilarion Hilarius, she blames herself and forgives him.

Sometimes the woman is stigmatized without actually being a character in a text. Alexis opens *Compère Général Soleil* with a metaphor for poverty in these terms—a crazy, enraged, skinny woman, a mother of whores and assassins, and a witch. In the *Repeating Island,* critic Antonio Benitez-Rojo perceives the Black Atlantic as the product of the rape of the Caribbean, figured as a woman:

> the Atlantic is the Atlantic (with all its port cities) because it was once engendered by the copulation of Europe—that insatiable solar bull— with the Caribbean archipelago; the Atlantic is today the Atlantic (the navel of capitalism) because Europe in its mercantile laboratory, conceived the project of inseminating the Caribbean womb with the blood of Africa; the Atlantic is today the Atlantic (NATO, World Bank, New York Stock Exchange, European Economic Community, etc.) because it was the painfully delivered child of the Caribbean, whose vagina was stretched between continental clamps . . . all Europe pulling on the forceps to help at the birth of the Atlantic. (5)

In conclusion, racism and sexism can inform representations of black women. Their bodies are eroticized, romanticized, objectified—in a word, marginalized. In subsequent chapters, I will demonstrate the ways in which women storytellers and authors rewrite the script offered by orature, literature, the media, and popular culture. Moving from object to subject, from the margin to the center to tell their *own* stories, women writers and characters collaborate in "double auteur(ité)." Simon Gikandi is on the mark in that he perceives a twofold process in which Caribbean women writers revise "the project of their male precursors who had in turn, revised and dispersed the colonial canon" (32). In chapter 3 I will examine women's inscription of women's voices.

3

Appropriate(d) Orature

Contes d'initiation féminine du pays Bassa
and Pluie et vent sur Télumée Miracle

Comme j'aurais aimé écrire, moi aussi! Il me semble que si je savais
écrire et lire ma vie serait différente.

(How I would have loved to write! It seems to me that if I knew how to
read and write my life would be different.)

Maryse Condé, La migration des coeurs

Yet so many of the stories that I write, that we all write, are my mother's
stories.

Alice Walker, In Search of Our Mothers' Gardens

According to critic Mae Gwendolyn Henderson, "it is not that black
women, in the past, have had nothing to say, but rather they have had no
say" (24). Maryse Condé affirms that "Whenever women speak out, they
displease, shock, or disturb" ("Order" 131). Prize-winning novelist Mariama Bâ also articulated the necessity for women to tell their own stories:
"Et pourtant, comme elles ont à dire et à écrire!" (and yet, they have so
much to tell and to write!) ("Fonction" 6). According to Bâ, these long
dormant stories would not only subvert those told by others but would
also function to liberate women. Her notion of telling and writing is central to my argument that female authors appropriate orality, permitting
their women characters to "have their say." Consequently, the inscription
of women's voices—the narrators' as well as the authors'—produces dual
female authorship ("double auteur(ité)"), which not only wrests women's
experiences from others' representations but is empowering for both, conferring authority on both narrator and writer.

The construction of black women as silent and the lack of access to
publishers have led Carole Boyce Davies and Elaine Savory Fido to use the
metaphor of voicelessness to describe the absence of Caribbean women
writers from the literary scene.[1] Florence Stratton labels this lack "exclu-
sionary practices"(1). Trinh T. Minh-ha addresses the issue to subvert si-

lence when she states that through writing "women have attempted to render noisy and audible all that had been silenced in phallocentric discourse" (37). Hélène Cixous's assertion that "a feminine text cannot fail to be more than subversive" (258) is relevant in this context also. Obioma Nnaemeka considers the choice of not to speak equally powerful ("Introduction" 4).

Some critics appropriate the female voice by naming their studies of black women: *Talking Back* (bell hooks), *Changing Our Own Words* (Cheryl Wall), *Francophone African Women Writers: Destroying the Emptiness of Silence* (Irène Assiba d'Almeida), *La parole des femmes* (Maryse Condé), *La parole aux Africaines* (Jean-Marie Volet) and *La parole aux négresses* (Awa Thiam), *Voix et visages de femmes dans les livres écrits par les femmes en Afrique francophone* (Madeleine Borgomano).[2]

In a global society, women's voices limited to the oral sphere are no longer sufficient. Urbanization has taken people away from rural areas, and certain modes of communication are impermanent and transitory. Weather can erase wall motifs. Names given to *pagnes* become outdated; the pattern entitled "Dallas," for example, was popular only while the television show was broadcast. Similarly, the original name of the *pagne,* called *conjoncture* during the economic crisis, was forgotten. Young women in Côte d'Ivoire can no longer decode the message inscribed on the "Kodjo laisse-moi dormir" cloth. Their mothers and grandmothers would know that the woman wearing it needs a rest from her husband, the red color of the pattern representing menstrual blood (Touré 132). The Caribbean headscarf, *madras,* has all but disappeared from contemporary Martinique and Guadeloupe, surfacing only in displays of traditional dress or at parades or pageants. In order for women's voices to be heard in the global arena, they now require access to the whole range of discourses, both oral and written. Aminata Sow Fall recognizes that it is her generation that is moving "du pilon à la machine à écrire" (from the pestle to the typewriter) (73–77). Mariama Bâ urges women to write in order to resist the inequality, oppression, and exploitation they experience:

> Plus qu'ailleurs, le contexte social africain étant caractérisé par l'inégalité criante entre l'homme et la femme, par l'exploitation et l'oppression séculaires et barbares du sexe dit faible, la femme-écrivain a une mission particulière. Elle doit, plus que ses pairs masculins, dresser un tableau de la condition de la femme africaine. Les injustices persistent, les ségrégations continuent malgré la décennie internationale dédiée à la femme par l'O.N.U., malgré les

beaux discours et les louables intentions. Dans la famille, dans les institutions, dans la rue, les lieux de travail, les assemblées politiques, les discriminations foisonnent. Les pesanteurs sociales étouffent dans leur cynique perpétration. Les moeurs et coutumes ajoutées à l'interprétation égoïste et abusive des religions font ployer lourdement l'échine. Les maternités incontrôlées vident les corps.

Comment ne pas prendre conscience de cet état de faits agressif? Comment ne pas être tenté de soulever ce lourd couvercle social? C'est à nous, femmes, de prendre notre destin en mains pour bouleverser l'ordre établit à notre détriment et ne point le subir. Nous devons user comme les hommes de cette arme, pacifique certes mais sûre, qu'est l'écriture.

(More than in other places, because the African social context is characterized by glaring inequality between men and women, by secular and barbaric exploitation and oppression of the "weaker" sex, the woman writer has a special mission. More than her male peers, she must paint a picture of the African woman's condition. Injustices persist and segregation continues in spite of the United Nations' International Decade of the Woman, and in spite of beautiful speeches and praiseworthy intentions. In the family, in the institutions, in the street, in the workplace, in political meetings, discrimination abounds. Social weights stifle in their cynical perpetration. Customs added to the egotistical and abusive interpretation of religions weigh heavily. Uncontrolled pregnancies empty the body.

How not be aware of this state of aggressive acts? How not be tempted to unload this heavy social burden? It is up to us, women, to take our destiny in hand in order to overturn the established order and not yield to it. We must, like men, use this peaceful but sure weapon, that is writing.) ("Fonction" 6–7)

Writing as a peaceful weapon will not only function to liberate women from oppressive customs, but also change their representation in literature. Bâ rejects specifically negritude writers' tendency to idealize the mother:

Les chants nostalgiques à la mère africaine confondue dans les angoisses d'homme à la Mère Afrique ne nous suffisent plus. Il faut donner dans la littérature africaine à la femme noire une dimension à la mesure de son engagement prouvé à côté de l'homme dans les batailles de libération, une dimension à la mesure de ses capacités démontrées dans le développement économique de notre pays. Cette place ne lui reviendra pas sans sa participation effective.

(Nostalgic songs to the African mother merged with man's anguish to Mother Africa are no longer sufficient. The black woman in African literature must be given a dimension that matches her proven involvement next to man in the battles for liberation, a dimension reflecting her abilities demonstrated in the economic development of our country. This place to which she is entitled will not be hers without her actual participation.) ("Fonction" 7)

What Bâ calls for is a complete revision of previous texts, which women writers try to do.

Critics agree that there is a link between oral and written narratives in Africa and the Caribbean, but they do not specifically deal with women's texts.[3] Many women writers from francophone Africa and the Caribbean do indeed link orality and writing. Werewere Liking refers to her novel *Elle sera de jaspe et de corail* as a *chant-roman* (song-novel) and critic Maximilien Laroche classifies Marie Chauvet's *Folie* as a *conte-roman* (tale-novel) (53). Simone Schwarz-Bart and Ina Césaire borrow the Ti-Jean character from Caribbean orature in *Ti-Jean L'horizon* (1979) and *L'enfant des passages ou la geste de Ti-Jean* (1988), respectively. Edwidge Danticat chooses the opening protocol for Haitian storytelling as the title of her collection of short stories *Krik? Krak!*, while Marie-Thérèse Colimon alludes to women's voices in the title of her collection *Le chant des sirènes* (1979). In Simone Schwarz-Bart's play *Ton beau capitaine,* the character Marie-Ange is represented exclusively through her voice which is recorded on a cassette.[4] Ina Césaire transformed the interviews she had with two elderly Martinican women into characters in her play *Mémoires d'isles.*[5]

Furthermore, I strongly believe that the predominance of first-person female narrators in texts by francophone African and Caribbean women is a deliberate strategy that reflects their desire for women to speak for themselves. Whether the writers are from Martinique, Guadeloupe, Haiti, Senegal, the Congo, or Cameroon that concern seems to be the same. Mayotte in Mayotte Capécia's *Je suis martiniquaise* (1948),[6] Télumée in Simone Schwarz-Bart's *Pluie et vent sur Télumée Miracle* (1972), Tituba in Maryse Condé's *Moi, Tituba sorcière . . .* (1986), Véronica and in Maryse Condé's *Hérémakhonon* (1976),[7] Zétou in Myriam Warner-Vieyra's *Le quimboiseur l'avait dit* (1980), ten-year-old Félicie in Gisèle Pineau's *Un papillon dans la cité* (1992), Zinnia in Lydie Dooh-Bunya's *La brise du jour*

(1977), Maïmouna in Maïmouna Abdoulaye's *Un cri du coeur* (1986), Angélique in Jeannette Balou-Tchichelle's *Coeur en exil* (1989), the unnamed narrator in Marie NDiaye's *La femme changée en bûche* (1989), Hermine (Mina) in Evelyne Mpoudi Ngolle's *Sous la cendre le feu* (1990), Sophie in Edwidge Danticat's *Breath, Eyes, Memory* (1995), Madjigeen in Fama Diagne Sène's *Le chant des ténèbres* (1997), Mégri and Saïda in Calixthe Beyala's *Seul le diable le savait* (1990) and *Les honneurs perdus* (1996) respectively, all relate their own stories.

Even the novels in the form of a diary or letters privilege the female voice. It seems as though these texts are meant to be read aloud. Mariotte in Simone and André Schwarz-Bart's *Un plat de porc aux bananes vertes* (1967) and Claudine in Nadine Magloire's *Le mal de vivre* (1967) are two examples. Myriam Warner-Vieyra's title character in *Juletane* (1982) writes a diary intended for her husband, but he dies before its completion. It is later found and read by Hélène Parpin. Similarly, Adeline Moravia's *Aude et ses fantômes* (1977), another novel in the form of a journal composed of three leather-bound volumes, is found in a desk drawer by the best friend of a woman who died in childbirth. Jacqueline Manicom's *La graine: Journal d'une sage-femme* (1974) reveals its diary structure in the title. Sidonie in Michèle Maillet's *L'étoile noire* (1990) prays that her diary will be read as testimony to her suffering. The narrators in Françoise Ega's *Lettres à une noire* (1978) and Mariama Bâ's *Une si longue lettre* (1979) engage in a simulated conversation with someone to whom the letters are never sent. Claire in Marie Chauvet's *Amour* (1968) finds voice through writing in her notebook.

Other novels present a more complex narrative structure imitating a conversation or storytelling session. Ken Bugul's *Cendres et braises* (1994) is in the form of a story told by adult Marie Ndiaga to her childhood friend Anta Seye. In Lilas Desquiron's *Les chemins de Loco-Miroir* (Reflections of Loko Miwa) (1990/1998) eighty-year-old Cocotte's voice opens the narrative, but beginning with chapter 2 her memories alternate with those of Violaine Dalavigne, born to an aristocratic family the same day. By the fifth chapter, it becomes clear that Gisèle Pineau's *La grande drive des esprits* (1993) is narrated by a female photographer who reconstructs the history of the descendants of Man Octavie from stories told to her by Léonce, Célestina, and Barnabé. In Calixthe Beyala's *C'est le soleil qui m'a brûlée* (The Sun Hath Looked upon Me) (1987/1996) the first-person narrator, Moi, speaks for and to the protagonist Ateba. In Beyala's *Tu t'appelleras Tanga* (Your Name Shall Be Tanga) (1988/1996), dying Tanga relates her story to her cellmate, Anna-Claude. Two voices alternate in Jan

J. Dominique's *Mémoire d'une amnésique* (1984), that of the first-person and a third-person narrator.

While *Léonora: L'histoire enfouie de la Guadeloupe* resists genre classification, residing in a space between autobiography and biography, the "author" Dany Bébel-Gisler takes pains to translate and transcribe from Creole Léonora's speaking voice, refashioning her words into French while situating them in an oral context. Bébel-Gisler's compatriot Maryse Condé confesses to a limited knowledge of and involvement in orality (Pfaff 160), nevertheless some of her novels demonstrate otherwise. The first volume of *Ségou* opens with a *griot*'s chant. The eponymous heroine of *Moi, Tituba, sorcière . . . noire de Salem* (I, Tituba, Black Witch of Salem) (1986/ 1992) proudly proclaims her identity as a witch and a black woman in the title. *La vie scélérate* (Tree of Life), whose French title is borrowed from a Creole proverb, is narrated in the first person by Claude Eloise Louis, who gives an oral account of her ancestors' lives. Its opening paragraph simulates a woman speaking with the identifying markers of orality, clarifications, digressions, lack of punctuation:

> Mon aïeul Albert Louis qui n'était encore l'aïeul de personne, mais un beau nègre d'environ trente-deux ans, je dis bien environ, car en ce temps-là, comme chacun sait, on ne se souciait guère d'état civil, simplement les gens de la plantation se rappelaient qu'il était né l'année du terrible cyclone qui avait couché arbres et cases d'un bout à l'autre de la Basse-Terre comme de la Grande-Terre et avait gonflé à la faire déborder cette paisible Sanguine qui ne faisait jamais que fournir à chacun assez d'eau pour remplir ses canaris et laver son linge bien blanc, beau, je répète, avec son crâne en forme d'oeuf, son menton creusé d'une fossette et sa bouche large s'ouvrant sur une infinité de dents à manger le monde. (13)

The English translation, which divides the paragraph into three complete sentences, unfortunately, eliminates some of those markers:

> My forebear Albert Louis was not yet the forebear of anyone that day but a handsome Negro of around thirty-two years of age. I say *around,* for, as everyone knows, they paid scant attention to birth certificates in those times. The people of the plantation simply remembered his being born in the year of the terrible hurricane that downed trees and cabins from one end to the other of both Basse- and Grande-Terre and swelled to overflowing the tranquil Sanguine, which usually provided the islanders with just enough water to fill their water jars and wash their clothes nicely white. So that day,

Albert Louis, handsome as I said, with his egg-shaped skull, chin marked by a dimple and wide mouth opening onto an infinity of teeth made for devouring the world. (3)

The closing paragraph returns the reader to the first paragraph, reminding him or her of the circumstances: "Et d'ailleurs saurais-je faire mentir le sang de toute ma lignée—et c'est là l'autre aspect de cette histoire, mon histoire—depuis mon aïeul Albert avec ses belles dents à manger le monde" (And anyway, how could I deny the blood of my entire ancestry—and this is the other aspect of this story, my story—beginning with my forebear Albert with his fine teeth made for devouring the world [348–49/367]).

Both *Traversée de la mangrove* (Crossing the Mangrove) and *La migration des coeurs* (Windward Heights) have multiple first-person narrators, most of whom are women. *Traversée de la mangrove* has seven—Mira, Man Sonson, Dinah, Léocadie, Rosa, Vilma, and Dodose—who during Francis Sancher's wake present their version of his life. *La migration des coeurs* has eleven *récits de femmes,* or women's narratives, recounted by Nelly Raboteur, Lucinda Lucius, Irmine, Julie, Sanjita, Etiennise, Sandrine, Romaine, and Ada. What is most important is that in each of the narratives, women's voices are meticulously inscribed.

Similarly, Werewere Liking and Marie-José Hourantier appropriate orature by translating and transcribing women's voices in *Contes d'initiation féminine du pays Bassa* (1981) two stories that were originally told by Bassa women during girls' initiation ceremonies in south central Cameroon. Designed to prepare girls for adulthood and marriage by teaching them about relationships between men and women, among women, and between adults and society, these stories represent the transmission of knowledge from one generation to the next. It is established in the introduction that, in fact, the first story, "Nguessi Ngonda," which I will analyze in this chapter, was passed down from mother to daughter. I was struck by how different this story was from the more well-known oral tales I examined in chapter 1, and became convinced that women's stories to women could be considered the foundation of women's writings.

Women characters in "Nguessi Ngonda" are not marginalized, objectified, or victimized, but are at the center of their own stories and become empowered through cooperation with other women. Although it is impossible to establish precise authorship, the storytellers as well as the target audience were exclusively female, engendering a safe space where they could express themselves freely. What Patricia Hill Collins ascertains about African American women finding a voice in their own groups and organizations is applicable in this context. Although the initiation rituals are no longer performed, this surviving women's story discloses much about how Bassa women viewed themselves and, furthermore, provides a striking model for women's writings.[8]

Oral tales invite multiple interpretations, and "Nguessi Ngonda" is no exception. One way to approach it would be as a typical marriage-plot tale, but I would like to suggest another possible interpretation; a young woman chooses a husband over the objections of her father. That she is not punished for subverting the patriarchal order sets this tale apart from Birago Diop's well-known "Une commission" (The message), in which the narrator explains the power of the father over the daughter in the following manner:

> En matière de mariage, comme en toute chose, une jeune fille n'a qu'une volonté, la volonté de son père. C'est son père qui doit décider à qui elle appartiendra: à un prince, à un dioula riche ou à un simple badolo qui sue au soleil des champs; c'est à son père à dire s'il veut la donner en aumône à un puissant marabout ou à un tout petit talibé.

> (But in the matter of marriage, as in all things, a girl must submit to her father's will. It is her father who must decide whom she is to belong to: a prince, a rich "dioula" or a simple "badolo" who sweats in the fields in the sun; it is for her father to say if he wishes to bestow her on a powerful "marabout" or an insignificant "talibe.") (94/94)[9]

In "Nguessi Ngonda" the king, who has always confided in his daughter and groomed her to take his place after his death, still thwarts her desire to choose her own husband by imposing high demands on potential suitors, thereby discouraging them. The successful candidate must accomplish a series of tasks in a single day: clear a huge forest; plant various fruits; and then harvest, cook, and serve the fruit to the king's family. Using her intelligence and magical powers, as well as the assistance of other women, Nguessi Ngonda aids her intended Johnny Waka in completing these tasks. In the process, she triumphs over two symbols of authority—her father as well as the army chief in charge of her capture.

Interestingly, compared to many other oral stories, gender roles seem to be reversed in this tale. It is Nguessi Ngonda who is clever and resourceful, while the object of her affection, Johnny Waka, is passive, fatalistic, and dependent on her. His masculine authority in this story is replaced by that of a female: "As-tu le pouvoir de réaliser ce que je te demanderai! As-tu la volonté de m'obéir?" (Do you have the power to accomplish what I will ask of you? Do you have the will to obey me?) (11). Johnny Waka falls asleep, a sign of defeat, when he realizes the impossibility of fulfilling her father's requirements within the allotted amount of time. It is Nguessi Ngonda who designs a plan that involves self-sacrifice. She instructs Johnny Waka about how to split her body in two with her magic wand. Later, when the king imposes an additional task—Johnny Waka must slay a dragon with an iron thread—it is Nguessi Ngonda who responds to a resigned Johnny Waka by once again giving him specific directions to follow. Even then, he falls short and puts their lives in danger. When the tests are successfully passed, the king suspects that his daughter and her fiancé have deceived him and orders them imprisoned, to be killed the following day. Again, Nguessi Ngonda takes the initiative and devises an escape plan. This series of rescues by a young woman who is not a mother are indeed rare in orature. At one point the female narrator wonders if Johnny Waka is worthy of Nguessi Ngonda: "C'était vraiment pour cet individu qu'elle allait mourir?" (Was it really for this individual that she was going to die?) (15).

In fact, all the males in this story are characterized by their physical or psychological shortcomings: a crippled old man appears briefly; Nguessi Ngonda's father does not keep his word; the army chief forgets the king's orders; afraid of animals, Johnny Waka chooses the wrong horse to escape, is bitten by a snake, and inadvertently puts lives in danger when he does not follow Nguessi Ngonda's exact instructions. Only one man, the second king who imprisons the fleeing couple until they can correctly solve his riddle, keeps his word at the end of the story. He relinquishes his crown to Johnny Waka. The women characters are not submissive as they are in male-centered stories, but active, healthy, admirable, generous, and even noble. For example, it is a woman who cures Johnny Waka's snakebite, and another woman is responsible for Nguessi Ngonda and Johnny Waka being freed from prison. In each case, the women characters have to subvert patriarchal authority in order to fulfill the community's expectations that they become wives and mothers. It is Nguessi Ngonda's father who attempts to disrupt that tradition by indirectly blocking her path to marriage. Actually, male/female complementarity is stressed as evidenced by the happy ending: Johnny Waka becomes king, with three happy co-wives who conceive and give birth to sons the same day.

In male-centered stories, the taking of a second wife is instigated by the husband to satisfy his own needs. The impetus for polygamy in "Nguessi Ngonda," however, lies elsewhere, with the women characters. Nguessi Ngonda's future co-wives are so impressed with her that they ask to join *her* household. She does not accept them readily, however; each must earn her place in the family. The second wife proves herself worthy by curing Johnny Waka's snakebite. The third woman, a queen, earns the rank of Nguessi Ngonda's co-wife by providing the answers to the riddles that will free Johnny Waka and her from prison. Releasing Nguessi Ngonda first and inviting her home to talk and share a meal, the queen is greatly impressed that Nguessi Ngonda divides the food into equal portions for her co-wife, husband, and host. The queen offers to provide the answers to the king's riddles, which in turn will free the whole family. Although Nguessi Ngonda, as the senior wife, has the power to accept or deny the queen's request to join the family as the third wife, she insists on consulting her young co-wife. It is significant that these negotiations occur in the particular place in the kitchen—"sous la claie"—where a woman keeps her private things and to which men are denied access. The king's wife subsequently brings Nguessi Ngonda's co-wife "sous la claie" where all three women "concluaient l'affaire" (conclude the matter) (24). These scenes are consistent with the bonding scenes that Mary Helen Washington finds in African American women's narratives (xxi).

The lesson of this tale, which celebrates women's power and their ability to "shape" men, is stated explicitly at the close. "Voyez-vous pourquoi une femme peut épouser n'importe quel homme? En vérité, s'il est bête, il devient intelligent; et s'il est animal, il devient humain, il suffit qu'elle le désire" (Do you see why a woman can marry any man? Truthfully, if he is stupid, he becomes intelligent; and if he is an animal, he becomes human. It is sufficient that she want him) (25). In order to achieve her goal, in this case, marriage, Nguessi Ngonda must take control so that her intended may pass the series of tests (clear the forest, slay the dragon, etc.). Even when additional obstacles are thrown in Johnny Waka's path, each one must be overcome as a rite of passage. In this sense, "Nguessi Ngonda" is an initiation story with the structure of a dilemma tale, which always ends with a question (Bascom). The audience is asked to decide through a subsequent discussion which one of the three sons by the three co-wives should be the rightful heir. The listeners are not asked to decide if the Nguessi Ngonda should be punished.

Magical intervention aids Nguessi Ngonda in her escape. Using her slingshot, she transforms her horse into a river, Johnny Waka into a canoe, and herself into a fisherman in order to evade capture by the army chief. Breaking an egg allows her to construct a temporary barrier—in the form of darkness, an ocean, a mountain, a fence—between herself and her pursuers. The young co-wife also has access to special healing powers. She revives Johnny Waka with a concoction made from leaves' sap that she drops into his eye, ear, and nostril, followed by a slap on the head, and by breathing into his mouth. In each case, women's initiative and intelligence coupled with magical powers allow them to triumph over adversity.

In translating and transcribing the stories, Liking and Hourantier made an effort to capture the oral quality of a performance—that is, inscribe speaking voices. They have kept the repetitions ("le même jour" [the same day], "une maison qui ne touchait ni le ciel ni la terre" [a house that touched neither the sky nor the ground]); refrains; onomatopoeias (the sound of the slingshot, of simmering pots, of horses' hooves); exclamations ("èèè"); series of questions, proverbs, and maxims; rhythmical language; and call-and-response structure between the storyteller and audience members (the storyteller says "Anguinguilaye" to keep the attention of the listeners who respond "Yessè).

Many of the characteristics of the oral performance maintained by Liking and Hourantier are transcribed in the Bassa language, not French. It could be their way of acknowledging the text's origins. Although their names appear on the cover and title page, they do not claim authorship of the narrative. What Maximilien Laroche posits concerning Caribbean tales, that the *conteur* is actually a mediator of the *supernarrateur,* the one who told the story long ago, is relevant here: "le conteur qui parle d'une double voix, raconte en stéréophonie une histoire à double signification: passée et présente, lointaine et proche"(the storyteller who speaks with a double voice, tells stereophonically a story with two significations: past and present, far away and near) (52). A dialogue is thus created between the *supernarratrice,* and the contemporary storyteller. Hourantier and Liking occupy still another space, that of transcriber.

The salient points in "Nguessi Ngonda" that appear in texts by contemporary African and Caribbean women are issues such as female identity, power, desire, marriage and children, gender relations, and cooperation among women, subverting the message in stories for the general public that show women as jealous, powerless, and passive. Herstory takes center stage in a context informed by women-produced orature.

Walter Ong states in *Orality and Literacy* that due to an education that focused less on rhetoric, women writers' texts are "more conversational than a platform performance" (159–60). His thesis is based on European women's experience, but for African and Caribbean writers, in general, it is a question of an appropriation of orality, a reclaiming of the oral tradition. Edouard Glissant in *Le discours antillais* and Jean Bernabé, Patrick Chamoiseau, and Raphaël Confiant in *Eloge de la créolité* have called for the creation of a new Caribbean literature informed by orality. As I stated earlier, women writers, especially, choose first-person narrators in order to privilege the female voice. Although Simone Schwarz-Bart is from Guadeloupe, *Pluie et vent sur Télumée Miracle* (The Bridge of Beyond) has much in common with the Cameroonian tale "Nguessi Ngonda." In addition to the centering on issues concerning women's culture, there is an emphasis on the intergenerational oral transmission of knowledge.

Pluie et vent has much in common with the structure and performance of a *conte,* in which the narrator begins by placing the protagonist within his or her family context. As in the other oral stories from the Caribbean, the connection is made to the foremothers, but in *Pluie et vent* they do not disappear after giving birth, but play an integral part in this story.[10] Before focusing on her own life, Télumée establishes the genealogy of her ancestors: Minerve, Toussine, and Victoire—her great-grandmother, grandmother, and mother, respectively. All have names that suggest majesty and mythology. Minerve, which calls to mind the Roman goddess of wisdom, has her status as the founder of the clan inscribed in her name, Minerve: "mère" or "mother." Toussine, called Reine (Queen) by her neighbors because of her aristocratic manner, earns the name Reine Sans Nom, or Queen Without a Name, as a sign of respect when she survives an extremely difficult time in her life. The name Victoire, which suggests triumph, is reinscribed throughout the text.[11] Télumée's half-sister Régina's name suggests royalty. Male ancestors are not exempt from this symbolic naming strategy. Xango, Toussine's stepfather, is also the name of a Yoruba deity. Jérémie, Toussine's husband, shares his name with the biblical prophet Jeremiah. Angebert, Télumée's father, displays his "angel-like" qualities when he rescues Victoire. All of these characters are metaphorically valorized through their names. It is completely ironic, however, that the narrator evokes the same nobility, glory, and grandeur when she speaks of "mother" France.

Pluie et vent has also been called a quest story, but because of the novel's Caribbean context with African roots, I prefer to see it more specifically as a woman's initiation tale that involves a journey and many trials. Like Nguessi Ngonda, who flees her father's house and travels from place to place, young Télumée is also separated from her immediate family. Her first displacement, the all-day trip on foot to her grandmother's house in Fond-Zombi, involves crossing drought-stricken land and a rotting floating bridge. The journey itself presages her new life as her grandmother grips her hand, and with the other holds onto the rusty cable as they cross to the other side (L'Autre Bord). Télumée will undergo several other displacements. As a teenager, she lives for a while at the Belle-Feuille plantation, where she is employed as a domestic, later returns to Fond-Zombi, then settles in La Folie, lives for a short time in Bel Navire, Bois Rouge, La Roncière, and Pointe-à-Pitre, and finally finds peace in La Ramée in her old age. This *errance,* which Edouard Glissant defines as alienation from the land (*Caribbean Discourse* 105–6), is opposed to a desired *enracinement.* Each move—whether voluntary or involuntary—brings new experiences and challenges that Télumée must negotiate. Each trial is overseen by an older woman who provides direction: her grandmother Reine Sans Nom or Toussine, followed by mentors Man Cia and Olympe.

Télumée's first trial occurs when at age ten she is expelled from her mother's house when she takes in a new lover. Fearing future competition, Victoire sends Télumée to live with Toussine in Fond-Zombi, where Télumée feels protected by her grandmother's skirt, "à l'abri de toutes les choses connues et inconnues" (safe from everything known and unknown) (47/40). At her grandmother's, Télumée participates in women's culture, from hair braiding to hygiene, from fashion to bonding. Reine Sans Nom's cabin is the site of special nurturing, the kind that many African American women writers describe (hooks, *Yearning,* 41–42). The two enjoy looking into each others' eyes, thus the one-way male gaze is transformed into a reciprocal one (Scharfman). Even after Toussine's death she remains a presence in her granddaughter's life. Télumée lives in her house, having it transported to a new place. She also sits in Toussine's rocking chair and wears her *madras* around her hips for support.

The serenity of life with Toussine, however, is disrupted when their perilous economic situation mandates a change. Reluctantly, Toussine sends teenage Télumée to the Belle-Feuille plantation to work for a rich *béké* family as a cook and housekeeper. The Desaragnes, whose name in French suggests a spider (araignée), assume unrestricted access to her body. Madame only grudgingly allows her time off on certain Sunday afternoons to visit her grandmother. Not only does she constantly give orders, Madame Desaragne flaunts her long blond hair, "comme pour me dire: où sont tes cheveux, négresse, pour qu'ils te caressent le dos" (as if to say, where's your hair, black girl, hanging down behind?) (94/89). Monsieur Desaragne, considering Télumée's body another commodity that he owns, offers her a silk dress as compensation for his sexual gratification. When Télumée refuses to sleep with him, he persists. She resists his advances with calm words, but when that strategy does not work, she brandishes her nails until Monsieur backs down. Although Télumée's vulnerability as a black woman is emphasized in this episode, she survives this second test by remembering her grandmother's teachings.

Returning to Fond-Zombi, she marries childhood sweetheart Elie. Life is fulfilling until his skills as a sawyer are no longer needed. Unemployment leads to infidelity, alcohol abuse, and domestic violence. Télumée passes this third test with the direct help of Reine Sans Nom, who bathes her wounds and takes her in when Elie throws her out. Télumée falls into a depression, but recovers.

After her grandmother's death, her best friend assumes the role of mentor. Man Cia, a healer, takes Télumée into the forest and initiates her into the secrets of plants, leaves, herbs, and the human body. The baths Man Cia prepares for Télumée on Sundays recall the ones Reine Sans Nom prepared for her granddaughter. This profession of healer will help Télumée later on.

Hard economic times return when Man Cia disappears, leaving Télumée no choice but to work in the dreaded cane fields. Olympe helps her overcome this fourth test. She shows Télumée how to protect herself from the brambles by bandaging her arms and legs. That Télumée cuts directly behind Olympe illustrates that this is indeed a mentoring relationship. This friendship, however, has a negative consequence that will lead to a fifth trial. Both Olympe and Télumée, leading hopeless lives, frequent bars together and get drunk on Sundays, conduct that scandalizes the town. In this way, Télumée repeats her mother's behavior in response to her abandonment by Hubert years earlier. That rum is what they drink is symbolic in that the women are trying to appropriate the fruits of their own labor. Their inability to handle the liquor illustrates their lack of success and repeats Elie's failure in the same area.

Longtime friend Amboise assists Télumée in overcoming this difficult trial. He follows her into the bar one day but leaves his tobacco pouch on the table along with an untouched glass of rum. This symbolic gesture marks the beginning of Télumée's recovery. They eventually move in together as equals. Amboise, who is older than Télumée, plays a similar role in the life of Télumée, as had Toussine, Man Cia, and Olympe.

Télumée's final two trials occur during the period after Amboise's violent death, when she, a popular healer, cures sick animals as well as an ailing five-year-old girl, Sonore, who was brought to her by her mother. Ange Médard, who everyone shuns and whom Télumée befriends, betrays Télumée by turning Sonore against her and returning her to her village without Télumée's knowledge or permission.[12] Then, one night, drunk, Ange Médard breaks into her house, destroys furniture, and threatens her with a knife. Expecting trouble, Télumée had purchased a pair of scissors and placed them on her stomach, one way to neutralize the nefarious effects of a *soukounyan*.[13] This episode invites comparison with the one in which Monsieur Desaragne came to her room years earlier. The innocent teenager was not expecting an invasion of her private space and thus had no weapon to protect herself. This time, with scissors lying on her womb, the mature adult's body becomes the site of resistance. Télumée does not have to use her weapon, however. Ange Médard trips on a table and impales himself. Télumée reacts by wiping his brow and comforting him. It is after this final test that the narrator earns the name Télumée Miracle—or Télumée, Miracle Woman. Not only has she survived the vicissitudes of life, but she has done so with authority as well as compassion.[14]

In addition to the characteristics of an initiation tale, there are other aspects of *Pluie et vent* that tie it to the oral tradition. While the novel spans five generations of the Lougandor family, approximately one hundred years beginning with the abolition of slavery in 1848, there are no references to specific dates, which reminds of us Antonio Benitez-Rojo's assertion that Caribbean culture "unfolds irregularly and resists being captured by the cycles of clock and calendar."[15] This atmosphere of timelessness also serves to heighten the text's affinity with the *conte*.

It is apparent from the outset that *Pluie et vent* assumes a listening audience. The text opens (and closes) on Télumée standing in her garden, relating the events of her life to an unseen audience. Throughout the narrative she addresses the listener/reader directly, a deliberate narrative strategy by Simone Schwarz-Bart, who in an interview said that she modeled fictional Télumée after the real-life Stéphanie Priccin, or Fanotte, a woman who used to organize evening storytelling sessions for the neighborhood youth in order to make them aware of the past. Although "sa vie résumait toute une fresque, toute une tranche de la vie des Antillais" (her life summarized a whole fresco, a slice of Antillean life), the youth showed little interest in what she had to say (15). The passage to writing, which also involves a translation from Creole to French and a transition from a collective audience to a single *destinataire,* is marvelously accomplished by Schwarz-Bart, who sees herself in the long line of women storytellers (Green 130–33). Télumée could not conceivably record her own story, seeing that she only attended elementary school. Schwarz-Bart, then, in transcribing Télumée's narrative, serves as the unrepresented recorder of Télumée's story, all the while deliberately preserving the components of an oral performance: proverbs, songs, rhythmical language.

As I mentioned above, Télumée gives the impression that she is narrating aloud a story, as others, principally her grandmother, had done before her. This oral transmission of history is evident from the second paragraph, which contains several verbs that emphasize speech: "Dans mon enfance, ma mère Victoire me *parlait* souvent de mon aïeule, la négresse Toussine. Elle en *parlait* avec ferveur et vénération, car, *disait*-elle (When I was a child, my mother Victory, often *talked* to me about my grandmother Toussine. She *spoke* of her with fervor and veneration: Toussine, she'd *say*) (emphasis added, 11/3). Télumée is also able to reconstruct that history with the help of others: "Selon ce qu'on me *dit*, plus de vingt ans après l'événement" (According to what I was *told* more than twenty years after the event) (emphasis added, 36/28). Learning from her grandmother who is illiterate takes place similarly: "Me l'avait-elle assez *répété,* Reine Sans Nom, que toutes les rivières descendent et se noient dans la mer, me l'avait-elle assez *répété?*" (How often had Queen Without a Name *told* me that all rivers go down to and are drowned in the sea, how often had she *told* me?) (emphasis added, 81/75). Much of what Toussine teaches Télumée about women's culture is in the form of proverbs or maxims: "La femme qui a ri est celle-là même qui va pleurer, et c'est pourquoi on sait déjà, à la façon dont une femme est heureuse quel maintien elle aura devant l'adversité" (The woman who has laughed is the same one as she will cry, and that is why one knows already, from the way a woman is happy, how she will behave in the face of adversity) (153/148); "si lourds que soient les seins d'une femme, sa poitrine est toujours assez forte pour les supporter" (However heavy a woman's breasts, her chest is always strong enough to carry them) (24–25/17).

There are other oral stories that are related within the main narrative. Old Abel plays the role of *conteur* as he explains to his bar patrons the origin of the scar on his arm: Man Cia, who transformed herself first into a huge bird, then into a large horse, scratched him with her hoof, leaving a scar that stretched from his wrist to his elbow. Reine Sans Nom is a particularly gifted storyteller. Every Thursday evening with young Télumée and Elie at her feet, she would preside over a storytelling session. Télumée reproduces the experience by quoting her grandmother's opening and closing protocol, which requires a response from the listeners. The last story told was always "L'homme qui vivait à l'odeur," curiously translated into English as "The Man Who Tried to Live on Air." It teaches a lesson about the importance of controlling one's own life; the moral is "the horse mustn't ride you, you must ride it." That Toussine routinely tells the story indicates that she understands its importance. But will the two young listeners—Télumée and Elie—internalize the message? There is a definite split along gender lines. It is no mere coincidence that the tale has a male protagonist, because it is Elie who reproduces Wvabor Hautes Jambes's mistakes. Wvabor, handsome and spoiled, lets his horse, Mes Deux Yeux, lead. After passing through many countries, he tries to dismount when he spots a beautiful woman. The horse, however, does not stop and Wvabor is never seen again, "la bête était devenue son maître" (the animal had become his master) (78/71). Like the man in the tale, Elie rides into town on a horse and the horse figuratively ends up riding him. Unemployment leaves Elie a broken man, and he never recovers. Conversely, as a child, Télumée benefited from the constant repetition of this tale and the discussion of its implications with her grandmother on Thursday nights after Elie returned home. As an adult, "ces marques d'attention contribuaient à me remettre en scelle, à me faire tenir en main les brides de mon cheval" (these marks of attention helped to lift me back in the saddle, to hold my horse's bridle with a firm grip) (169/164).

Another story related by her grandmother that Télumée recalls involves a bird who vows revenge against a young hunter if he kills it. Frightened, the hunter backs off when the bird uses its song as a defense. Télumée identifies with the bird, who triumphs over an armed foe: "Je . . . me prenais pour l'oiseau qu'aucune balle ne pouvait atteindre, car il conjurait la vie de son chant" (I took myself for the bird that couldn't be hit by any bullet because it invoked life with its song) (75/68). It is understandable then that Télumée's foremothers are also associated with birds: "Les Lougandor ont toujours aimé survoler, ils s'accrochaient des ailes et ils se hissaient" (The Lougandor family has always liked to fly high, grow wings, raise themselves up) (32/24). Singing as a form of resistance also figures in *Pluie et vent* among cane workers, Victoire, Reine Sans Nom, and Télumée, who use it as a means of escape from tedious work.

Not only does Télumée experience the lessons of these tales, but as an adult passes on these stories and songs to Sonore, the girl left in her care, who in the evening would sit on her lap and listen attentively. The intergenerational oral transmission of knowledge is thus maintained. Télumée is also sure to include stories about female heroines like la Mulâtresse Solitude, who fought against the reimposition of slavery. This reliance on memory—"J'avais toujours entendu dire" (I'd always heard it said that) (176/172)—is crucial for those whose collective story has not been recorded.

It follows, then, that spoken words have special power. According to Toussine, they have the ability to calm an agitated man. Télumée finds Amboise's voice peaceful and reassuring. It is Amboise's ability to speak Creole and French and consequently, communicate their demands to management that lead the strikers to ask him to be their representative, their spokesperson. Women's voices are especially strong in *Pluie et vent*. Télumée is captivated by the mere sound of her grandmother's voice. Storytelling for Reine Sans Nom is an art that involves at least four senses. She has the ability to *feel* and *smell* her words; she creates visual images as music flows from her mouth: "Elle *sentait* ses mots, ses phrases, possédait l'art de les arranger en images et en sons, en musique pure, en exaltation" (She was conscious of her words, her phrases, and possessed the art of arranging them in images and sounds, in pure music, in exaltation) (emphasis added, 76/69). Not only is her grandmother good at storytelling, Télumée senses that she loves doing it *for* (French *pour* not *à* [to]) her and Elie. Although Télumée continues to feel the presence of her grandmother even after her death, "Je sus alors que la protection des morts ne remplace pas la voix des vivants" (the protection of the dead can't replace the voice of the living) (195/190).

On the other hand, whites' words have a different function. They are nostalgic and harmful. The Desaragnes, for whom Télumée works, dream of the "good old days" of plantation life. Listening to their racist and condescending words, Télumée appears to remain passive but imagines a countercharge: "je prenais ces paroles et m'asseyais de tout mon vaillant poids sur elles, paroles de blanc, rien que ça" (I took the words and sat on them with all my sturdy weight—white man's words, that's all) (93/87). Another form of resistance is escaping to her own safe space: "Je me faufilais à travers ces paroles comme si je nageais dans l'eau la plus claire qui soit, sentant sur ma nuque, mes mollets, mes bras" (I glided in and out between the words as if I were swimming in the clearest water, feeling the cooling breeze on my neck, my arms, the back of my legs) (94/88).[16] Nature is also an ally: "un vent s'emparait des paroles de Madame Desaragne, et les déposait sur la montagne Balata, à la cime des mahoganys où elles tintaient pour les oiseaux, pour les fourmis des arbres, pour Dieu, pour personne" (a wind caught up Madame Desaragne's words and dripped them on Balata mountain, on the tops of the mahoganies, where they rang out for the birds, the tree ants, for God, for nobody)(98/92). When Monsieur Desaragne comes to her room one night, Télumée resists his advances with calm words that he ignores. It is only when she brandishes her nails that he backs down. Her words alone have no power. It is understandable, then, why whites misinterpret the blacks' sorrow songs for joy.

Speech can exist in other forms. Old Tac-Tac refuses to use words to speak to his neighbors, yet each morning when he plays his bamboo flute, he creates a universal language: "il connaît toutes les langues de la terre, les langues comme elles doivent se parler" (he knows all the languages in the world, languages as they ought to be spoken) (197/193). According to Isidore Okpewho, the flute is a tone instrument found in African communities where tone languages are spoken, "and the idea is for the instrument to reproduce the tones of a statement almost exactly the way it would sound in normal speech" (255). Schwarz-Bart's inscription of Tac-Tac's "voice" in the following passage may seem to resemble rambling prose, but its three long sentences and abundance of onomatopoeias attempt to imitate the rhythms of speech—that is, Tac-Tac's flute:

> c'était Tac-Tac qui commençait à parler, selon son dire, toutes les langues de la terre. Et il soufflait de tout son corps par saccades, longue, brève, brève, longue, brève, longue, longue, longue, longue, longue qui traversaient la voûte de la forêt tout droit pour venir s'engouffrer dans nos poitrines, en frissons, en sanglots, en amour et ça vous soulevait comme ça de terre tout droit, quand vous ouvriez les yeux. Et c'est debout qu'il était, debout devant sa longue flûte de bambou et il n'y avait pas moyen de ne pas l'écouter, car ça ne faisait que rentrer: voum-tac, et ça vous retournait dans le même temps que vous ouvriez les yeux, et c'était ainsi, vous ne pouviez rien y faire, Tac-Tac s'envolait devant son bambou après avoir déversé tout ce qui l'avait rempli, tout ce qu'il avait senti, ce matin-là.

> (it was Tac-Tac starting to speak, according to him, all the languages on earth. And he blew with his whole body, in fits and starts—long, short, short, long, short, long, long, long, long, long—which traveled straight through the vault of the forest and into our bosoms, in shudders, in sobs, in love. And it lifted you straight up off the earth, as you opened your eyes. He was up already, standing up in front of his long bamboo flute, and you couldn't help hearing him, for it kept coming back—voum-tac, voum-tac—and it got you just as you were opening your eyes, and so there it was, nothing to be done, Tac-Tac took off with his bamboo, pouring out all that had filled him, all that he'd felt.) (188/184)

Tac-Tac's flute playing reconstructs the rhythms of speech. The language he produces is what Glissant would characterize as "le cri de la Plantation, transfiguré en parole du monde" (the cry of the Plantation, transfigured into the speech of the world) (*Poétique* 88/73).

Other forms of nonverbal communication associated specifically in the Caribbean with voice and inscription are the drum and the *lambi,* both instruments of resistance during the slave period, whose purpose was not forgotten after emancipation. As a survival strategy in *Pluie et vent,* Télumée is advised by Man Cia to be like a drum and allow one side to take the blows while the other side remains calm. The sounds that Amboise produces on his drum, like Tac-Tac's flute, have the capacity to convey his life's experiences. The lambi is used to rally the striking cane workers in their struggle against oppressive working conditions. Cowrie shells also mark the graves of the protesters who were killed and will forever serve as a reminder of their courage.

At the same time, some of these forms of communication can be inscribed. Amboise "*imprimait* à son tambour une détente" (printed a pause on his drum) (emphasis added, 209; my translation).[17] This site of male inscription is reminiscent of Jean-Marie Adiaffi's analogy of the drummer and writer. Reine Sans Nom "en détachant ses mots, comme pour les *graver* au fond de mon esprit" (detaching her words, as if to engrave them on my mind) (emphasis added, 79),[18] too recalls Clémentine Faik-Nzuji's assertion about graphic symbols, here inscribed by Toussine. Later, in explaining the invisible thread that connects all the homes of Fond-Zombi to Télumée, like a teacher using chalk on a blackboard, she traces the outline of Fond-Zombi on the ground with a dry branch. This is another form of writing.

Fertility and motherhood are not exalted in *Pluie et vent* as they are in male texts. Status is gained not by the number of children one has, nor is childlessness stigmatized. Economic deprivation, one legacy of slavery, causes Télumée to be relieved that she has no children of her own. Seeing whimpering and sleepy children clinging to their mother's skirts as they make their way to the cane fields before dawn, she remarks: "dans mon ventre ils étaient, agrippés à mes boyaux et c'est là qu'ils devaient rester, tout au fond de mes intestins jusqu'à nouvel ordre" (in my belly, hanging onto my guts, that's where they were, and that's where they'd stay until further orders) (199/194). This decision is not questioned in the text. Yet motherhood can occur without one actually giving birth. When Sonore is first handed to Télumée, she feels life move inside her. She goes on to raise Sonore as her grandmother Reine Sans Nom had raised her. "Othermothers" in *Pluie et vent* replace as well as supplement birth mothers, as they do in many African and Caribbean communities.

Télumée standing in her garden in La Ramée as the text opens and closes is significant. First, it situates her in a location that defines her gender, class, and age: "je préfère rêver, encore et encore, debout au milieu de mon jardin, comme le font toutes les vieilles de mon âge, jusqu'à ce que la mort me prenne dans mon rêve, avec toute ma joie" (I prefer to dream, on and on, standing in my garden, just like any other old woman of my age, till death comes and takes me as I dream, me and all my joy) (11/3). The text closes in a similar manner: "mais je mourrai là, comme je suis, debout, dans mon petit jardin, quelle joie!" (But I shall die here, where I am, standing in my little garden. What happiness!) (249/246). Second, as a refuge, like Alice Walker's mother's garden, it is a locus of peace and creativity. The beautiful flowers and vegetables from which Télumée derives so much happiness are one aspect of her cultural expression, an activity she had shared successively with Elie, Amboise, and Sonore as had grandmother Toussine and husband, Jérémie. The following passage, which describes the garden she tills with Amboise in La Folie, accentuates male/female complementarity in terms that suggest sexuality, conception, and birth:

> Nous aimions repiquer les repousses, relever les sillons, loger les semences au ventre de la terre. Notre parcelle descendait en pente douce jusqu'au creux du vallon, où coulait un ruisseau baptisé pompeusement du nom de ravine. Au bas de la pente venait une terre noire et huileuse à point, de celles destinées à mettre au jour de longues ignames, sèches et fondantes. La ravine proche nous donnait son eau, l'ombre de ses arbres. Amboise bêchait, cassait les mottes de terre que j'effritais en fine pluie entre mes doigts. D'année en année, ce lieu perdu nous retenait, nous sollicitait davantage. A mesure que notre sueur pénétrait cette terre, elle devenait nôtre, se mettait à l'odeur de nos corps, de notre fumée et de notre manger.

> (We enjoyed pricking out the seedlings, raising the furrows, setting the seeds in the womb of the earth. Our plot sloped gently down to the bottom of the valley, to a little stream grandly known as the torrent. At the bottom of the slope the earth was black and rich, just right for bringing forth long yams, crisp and juicy. The nearby torrent gave us its water and the shade of its trees. Amboise dug and broke up the clods of earth, and I crumbled them into a fine rain between my fingers. Every year this out-of-the-way place appealed to and attracted us more. As our sweat seeped into the soil, it became more and more ours, one with the odor of our bodies.) (211–12/ 208–9)

That *lougan*, which forms part of Télumée's family name— Lougandor— means "cultivated land" in Wolof reinforces our idea.[19] In addition to the garden as a metaphor of reproduction, it also serves as a private and safe place. Toussine and Jérémie made love there. Amboise and Télumée spend hours in their garden discussing various topics. This space is not gender specific, as was the site "sous la claie," where the women conducted their business in "Nguessi Ngonga." A woman working in her garden signals a return to health. When Toussine emerges from a self-imposed exile and is once again observed by the neighbors cutting down weeds and planting flowers and vegetables, it is an indication that she has recovered from the loss of her daughter Meranée and the destruction of the family home in a fire.

One can conclude then that the garden in this narrative functions as the antithesis of the cane fields, a site of loss and economic exploitation, where prickles, bees, hornets, and the oppressive heat threaten those who work there. The garden represents ownership, beauty, and voluntary work on a small plot of land whose cultivation provides nourishment, while the cane fields represent dispossession and tedious labor whose fruits the workers will not enjoy (the cane fields are adjacent to and owned by the sugar refinery). That Télumée remains standing at the end of *Pluie et vent* is a sign of endurance against the storms (pluie et vent) alluded to in the title.

Old Télumée, conscious of her race and gender, reflects on her past with no regrets. It is only looking back at the attempted rape by Monsieur Desaragne that she realizes: "ma victoire de négresse, ma victoire de femme" (the victory I'd won, as a Negro and as a woman) (112/106). During the journey back to Fond-Zombi after leaving the Desaragnes for good, she gazes at her reflection in the water:

> Je songeai que Dieu m'avait mise sur terre sans me demander si je voulais être femme, ni quelle couleur je préférais avoir. Ce n'était pas ma faute s'il m'avait donné une peau si noire que bleue, un visage qui ne ruisselait pas de beauté. Et cependant, j'en étais bien contente, et peut-être si l'on me donnait à choisir, maintenant, en cet instant précis, je choisirais cette même peau bleutée, ce même visage sans beauté ruisselante.

> (I thought God had put me on earth without asking me if I wanted to be a woman or what color I'd like to be. It wasn't my fault he'd given me a blue-black skin and a face not overflowing with beauty. And yet I was quite content; and perhaps, if I was given the choice, now, at this moment, I'd choose that same bluish skin, that same face not overflowing with beauty.) (116/110)

Not only are Lougandor women supposed to survive, they are expected to adapt, subvert, and resist. Toussine advises Télumée to take pride in being a woman:

ondule comme un filao, rayonne comme un flamboyant et craque, gémis comme un bambou, mais trouve ta démarche de femme et change de pas en vaillante, ma toute belle; et lorsque tu craqueras comme le bambou, lorsque tu soupireras de lassitude et de dégoût, gémis et désespère pour toi seule et n'oublie jamais qu'il y a une femme contente de vivre, sur la terre, quelque part.

(Sway like a filao, shine like a flame tree, creak and groan like a bamboo, but find your woman's walk and change to a valiant step, my beauty. And when you creak like a bamboo, when you sigh with weariness and disgust, when you groan and despair for yourself alone, never forget that somewhere, somewhere on earth there's a woman glad to be alive.) (121/115)

Conversely, the male characters in *Pluie et vent* experience an early death. Many die violently: Angebert is stabbed by Germain, Amboise is scalded by steam during a strike, Ange Médard is impaled. The sole male Lougandor heir dies when Victoire miscarries a fully formed fetus. These events lead Ernest Pépin to classify the male characters in *Pluie et vent* as either "géniteur, séducteur, sauveur, destructeur" (reproducer, seducer, savior, destroyer) (Pépin, "*Pluie et vent*" 98). Although many males are destroyed by the "pluie et vent" of life that the women successfully negotiate, Télumée, as a young woman, insists, "mais la balance penchait, me semblait-il, en faveur des hommes, et dans leur chute même ils conservaient quelque chose de victorieux" (But it seemed to me the balance was in favor of the men, and that even in their fall there was still something of victory) (71/64).

Pluie et vent treats the myriad aspects of women's experience—from the developing female body to its vulnerability through threats of sexual exploitation, from women's mutual support in times of crisis, to betrayal. Still, Télumée's young girlfriends are determined to surpass their models, thereby rewriting their scripts: "Avec leurs corps de femmes et leurs yeux d'enfants, mes camarades se sentaient toutes prêtes à malmener l'existence, elles entendaient conduire leur vie à bride abattue, rattraper leurs mères, leurs tantes, leurs marraines" (With their women's bodies and children's eyes, my friends felt quite ready to get the better of existence; they intended to lead their lives full tilt, to overtake their mothers and aunts and godmothers) (82/75–76). Télumée, in particular, watches all the women who died prematurely—"qui se perdaient avant l'heure, se désarticulaient, s'anéantissaient" (lost before their time, broken destroyed) (82/75) and wonders about her own future.

Schwarz-Bart sets out to demystify women's experience in *Pluie et vent* but ends up mythicizing it. The reputations of the Lougandor women reach epic proportions:

> Nous les Lougandor, nous ne sommes pas des coqs de race, nous sommes des coqs guinmes, des coqs de combat. Nous connaissons les arènes, la foule, la lutte, la mort. Nous connaissons la victoire et les yeux crevés. Tout cela ne nous a jamais empêchés de vivre, ne comptant ni sur le bonheur, ni sur le malheur pour exister.

> (We Lougandors are not pedigree cocks, we're fighting cocks. We know the ring, the crowd, fighting, death. We know victory and eyes gouged out. And all that has never stopped us from living, relying neither on happiness nor on sorrow for existence.) (120–21/115)

These characters not only survive, often without male support—one legacy of slavery—but hold their heads high and assure the telling of their own (his)tory of triumph to future generations. This is not simply Télumée's story, but that of her ancestors—Minerve, Reine Sans Nom, Victoire—as well as her descendant Sonore, and although she leaves town, the line is still unbroken.

The Lougandor legacy survives in written form as Schwarz-Bart acts as a *marqueuse de paroles*, or translator/transcriber, to narrator/*oralituraine* Télumée. *Pluie et vent*, a female initiation tale that she lived, subverts the male-centered oral and written narratives that I studied in earlier chapters in that it revisits the private women's oral stories like "Nguessi Ngonda," made available to the public through its inscription by Werewere Liking and Marie-José Hourantier, in which women triumph over adversity with the aid of other women, a pattern we will see in subsequent chapters. By inscribing female voices, especially storytellers, women writers confer authorship on them and assure their legacy of transmitting knowledge.

4

Inscribing Friendship

Mariama Bâ's *Une si longue lettre* and Michèle Maillet's *L'étoile noire*

Chère Pia! Je songeais à elle avec tendresse et gratitude. De penser qu'en toutes circonstances je pouvais compter sur elle et sur son indéfectible amitié.

(Dear Pia! I dreamed about her with tenderness and gratitude. To think that in any circumstance, I could count on her and her indestructible friendship.)

Lydie Dooh-Bunya, *La brise du jour*

Si la jouvencelle écrit? Sa voix, en dépit du silence, circule. Un papier. Un chiffon froissé. Une main de servante, dans le noir. Un enfant au secret. Le gardien devra veiller jour et nuit. L'écrit s'envolera par le patio, sera lancé d'une terrasse. Azur soudain trop vaste. Tout est à recommencer.

(And what if the maiden does write? Her voice, albeit silenced, will circulate. A scrap of paper. A crumpled cloth. A servant-girl's hand in the dark. A child, let into the secret. The jailer must keep watch day and night. The written word will take flight from the patio, will be tossed from a terrace. The blue of heaven is suddenly limitless. The precautions have all been in vain.)

Assia Djebar, *L'amour, la fantasia*

In the previous chapter, I argued that some women writers position their rural women characters at the center of their own initiation tales, which depict the ways in which women become empowered when they negotiate life's vicissitudes and triumph over adversity. The values and experiences expressed by these women's voices—Télumée's and the anonymous authors and transmitters of "Nguessi Ngonda"—are informed, in part, by gender. Furthermore, what they articulate is directed specifically to succeeding generations. These "oralituraines" are transformed into authors by Schwarz-Bart and Liking and Hourantier. In this chapter, I will show that urban middle-class women characters appear to be, in this way, heirs to Nguessi Ngonda and Télumée as both character and text. One major difference, however, is that the protagonists of Mariama Bâ's *Une si longue lettre* (So Long a Letter) (1979) and Michèle Maillet's *L'étoile noire* (1990) inscribe their own voices.

The narrators and "authors" of *Une si longue lettre* and *L'étoile noire* are physically confined for religious reasons. Ramatoulaye observes Islamic custom, which requires that widows remain at home for a fixed period of time, while Sidonie is arrested along with her Jewish employers in France and imprisoned in a concentration camp. While the justification for and circumstances of the confinement are certainly not comparable—one is based on respect for religion, the other, on hatred—both Ramatoulaye and Sidonie keep a diary in which they record their pain and the role of friendship in survival. In addition, the voice that each character inscribes, her own, participates in a dialogue with someone else. Each diary has a distinct narratee other than its writer: *Une si longue lettre* is addressed to Aïssatou, Ramatoulaye's best friend, and Sidonie's diary is a testimonial to future generations.

That narratives by women celebrate women's close friendships is a fact that mirrors reality. Janice Raymond creates the term *gyn/affection* to describe commitment, bonding, sharing secrets and confidences, and listening to one another. Patricia Hill Collins in *Black Feminist Thought* locates three "safe spaces" where black women find a voice. One is among other women (96). The Hausa in West Africa have a special word—*kawaye*—that designates a woman's best friend (Mary Smith 56). It is not surprising that such a character is often found in women's narratives. Mary Helen Washington has identified a distinctly African American women's literary tradition in which "women talk to other women . . . and their friendships with other women—mothers, sisters, grandmothers, friends, lovers—are vital to their growth and well-being" (xxi). Washington has also isolated what she calls a bonding scene which I contend occurs frequently in texts by francophone African and Caribbean women. In "Nguessi Ngonda," for example, the title character and two co-wives together decide their future in such a place, "sous la claie," in the space in the kitchen reserved for women. In *Une si longue lettre*, Ramatoulaye and Aïssatou cement their friendship when, as playmates, they make the same wish while burying their baby teeth in the same hole. Although the relationships in *L'étoile noire* are among adult women in crisis, bonding and confiding are the means by which the women survive. In fact, one can say that in *Une si longue lettre* and *L'étoile noire* friendship structures each text.

Relationships between co-wives and intergenerational mentoring alliances, which are prevalent among women of African descent, are often represented in orature and literature. Women's friendships in Africa and the Caribbean resemble their American counterparts in that they are characterized by what Susan Koppelman labels mutuality and reciprocity.

Une si longue lettre is an elegy to women's friendship—from trust and belonging in childhood to material and emotional assistance during the adult years. Although the narrative is centered on Aïssatou's support of Ramatoulaye, reciprocity characterizes this relationship as well. Ramatoulaye had supported Aïssatou when she encountered opposition from her mother-in-law because of her "inferior caste status," and when she divorced Mawdo, refusing to accept sharing him with another wife. Three years later, Ramatoulaye is faced with a similar dilemma when her husband Modou abandons her and their twelve children to marry Binetou, a close friend of their teenage daughter. Aïssatou's support of Ramatoulaye includes the gift of a car to facilitate her getting around Dakar. Ramatoulaye learns to drive, principally, so as not to disappoint her friend. Rama expresses her appreciation and gratitude by contrasting lasting friendship to transitory love: "L'amitié a des grandeurs inconnues de l'amour. Elle se fortifie dans les difficultés, alors que les contraintes massacrent l'amour. Elle résiste au temps qui lasse et désunit les couples. Elle a des élévations inconnues de l'amour" (Friendship has splendours that love knows not. It grows stronger when crossed, whereas obstacles kill love. Friendship resists time, which wearies and severs couples. It has heights unknown to love) (79/54).[1]

One can say that this longstanding friendship—*wolëre* in Wolof—was passed down the female line from generation to generation. Ramatoulaye and Aïssatou's grandmothers and mothers used to exchange messages daily over the fence separating their two compounds. Their own friendship, fondly recalled by Ramatoulaye as the narrative opens, was solidified at a very young age as they shared mangoes. Ramatoulaye and Aïssatou were also students together at the Koranic school, French school, and the Ecole Normale; they became teachers, married friends Modou Fall and Mawdo Bâ, respectively, socialized, and took vacations together. Ramatoulaye even named one of her daughters and one of her sons after Aïssatou and Mawdo. Eldest daughter Daba calls Aïssatou "aunt." After many years of marriage, Ramatoulaye and Aïssatou both become single mothers when their husbands take much younger second wives. Their shared history makes empathy and unconditional support logical and understandable.

In *Une si longue lettre*, the women's friendship has outlasted their marriages and has been sustained over the years despite geographical distance: "Tu m'as souvent prouvé la supériorité de l'amitié sur l'amour. Le temps, la distance autant que les souvenirs communs ont consolidé nos liens et font de nos enfants, des frères et des soeurs" (You have often proved to me the superiority of friendship over love. Time, distance, as well as mutual memories have consolidated our ties and made our children brothers and sisters) (104–5/72). Ramatoulaye and Aïssatou communicate through writing, which sustains their friendship. Their mothers' and grandmothers' fence has been replaced by the Atlantic Ocean. The locus of this friendship is the paper on which Ramatoulaye writes. The page substitutes for a face-to-face conversation, which will have to wait until Aïssatou's next visit to Dakar. In the meantime, Aïssatou's contribution to the discussion is not completely unrepresented in the text. As reported by Ramatoulaye, she sends her a letter through the mail reminding her that the end of her confinement as a widow is approaching, and that it coincides with Aïssatou's imminent arrival. Ramatoulaye describes the salutary effect of her friend's correspondence in this way: "Ces mots caressants qui me décrispent" (These caressing words, which relax me) (104/71).

Ramatoulaye and Aïssatou were neighbors, educated in Senegal at the French school, who as adults reside on different continents and communicate through the mail. Also, in *Une si longue lettre* the *destinataire's* letters are not represented, thereby the illusion of a listener, a sounding board, is created. Rama's "chat" discloses that sharing plays a large role in their relationship: "Ta déception fut la mienne comme mon reniement fut le tien" (Your disappointment was mine, as my rejection was yours) (81/55).

The model of female solidarity provided by Ramatoulaye and Aïssatou is not lost on the younger generation. Daba, Ramatoulaye and Modou's oldest daughter, recognizes its importance when she scolds Dame Belle-mère, Binetou's mother, for breaking up her parents' marriage: "Comment une femme peut-elle saper le bonheur d'une autre femme? Tu ne mérites aucune pitié" (How can a woman sap the happiness of another? You deserve no pity) (103/71). Binetou, in fact, had been Daba's best friend. Daba's strong words are applicable to Tante Nabou as well, who, disapproving of her son's marriage to a *castée* (casted individual) plotted against her daughter-in-law Aïssatou by grooming her young niece and namesake, Petite Nabou, to be his second wife. Refusing to accept the new arrangement, Aïssatou leaves the marriage.

As I hinted above, Bâ reworks the epistolary form in *Une si longue lettre* so that it resembles a "speaking" diary. The first four sections of Ramatoulaye's "very long letter" to her friend Aïssatou consist of daily entries chronicling the events after her husband Modou's death. Chapters 5 through 15 are in effect a meditation on the past, while 17 through 28 return to the present. The text, however, never really abandons the immediacy of epistolary discourse. That the letter is never sent to the Senegalese embassy in Washington, D.C., where Aïssatou works, is immaterial. Obioma Nnaemaka correctly notes that Ramatoulaye's letter "is the exteriorization of an internal dialogue, a dialogue that the author wishes to share with the reader. The letter is, therefore, a pretext for a dialogue with the self" ("Mariama Bâ" 20). I would argue further that the dialogue extends to Aïssatou, whose voice is also evident in the text, a fact that will be discussed below.

During the course of the novel, Ramatoulaye's growth can be charted in two distinct stages, as a coming to speech and a coming to writing. The former is illustrated in two complementary scenes. The first occurs when the Imam, family friend Mawdo, and brother-in-law Tamsir arrive at her house one Sunday evening to announce Modou's second marriage. Although Ramatoulaye feels hurt and betrayed, she smiles, thanks them for the news, offers them something to drink, and shakes hands when they leave: "Je m'appliquais à endiguer mon remous intérieur" (I forced myself to check my inner agitation) (58/38). She does not want to give them the satisfaction of being able to detect and then tell others about her distress. After all, she had no idea that Modou was courting Binetou. Listening to their words—"gouttes de poison" (drops of poison) (57/37)—she recalls her mother's maxims in which she had warned her about Modou.

Five years later, however, when the same three men visit Ramatoulaye's house to commemorate the fortieth day of Modou's death, the tables are turned. Tamsir beckons the Imam and Mawdo to join him in Ramatoulaye's bedroom, where he announces that he will marry her. On the previous occasion Tamsir had done most of the talking, but this time Ramatoulaye breaks the silence imposed on her by society:

> Cette fois, je parlerai. Ma voix connaît trente années de silence, trente années de brimades. Elle éclate, violente, tantôt sarcastique, tantôt méprisante . . . "Tamsir, vomis tes rêves de conquérant. Ils ont duré quarante jours. Je ne serai jamais ta femme."

> (This time I shall speak out. My voice has known thirty years of silence, thirty years of harassment. It bursts out, violent, sometimes sarcastic, sometimes contemptuous . . . "Tamsir, purge yourself of your dreams of conquest. They have lasted forty days. I shall never be your wife.") (85–86/57–58)

Mawdo reacts to Ramatoulaye's unexpected outburst by demanding her silence: "Tais-toi! Tais-toi! Arrête! Arrête!" (Shut up! Shut up! Stop! Stop!)

(86/58). Reduced to silence, Tamsir, the Imam, and Mawdo leave. That Ramatoulaye's bedroom is the sight of her "prise de parole" is appropriate. They have, in fact, invaded her private space, and Tamsir's arrogant proposal breaks the laws of Islam. Her period of mourning is not complete. In addition, it is the youngest brother who is supposed to inherit his brother's widow. Ramatoulaye's refusal to become Tamsir's fourth wife is also informed by her concept of marriage as involving reciprocal love and choosing one's own partner. Her recovery of voice releases not only pent-up emotions, but precipitates a new phase in her life. At the close of her confinement, and obliged to circulate publicly, to pay bills and the like, Ramatoulaye dares to go to the movies alone. For a middle-aged Muslim Senegalese woman this is an audacious act.

Aïssatou had responded to the news of her husband Mawdo's marriage to Petite Nabou in writing, leaving the "lettre de rupture" on their bed. Interestingly, she touches on the same themes as Ramatoulaye:

Mawdo,

Les princes dominent leurs sentiments, pour honorer leurs devoirs. Les "autres" courbent leur nuque et acceptent en silence un sort qui les brime.

Voilà, schématiquement, le règlement intérieur de notre société avec ses clivages insensés. Je ne m'y soumettrai point. Au bonheur qui fut nôtre, je ne peux substituer celui que tu me proposes aujourd'hui. Tu veux dissocier l'Amour tout court et l'amour physique. Je te rétorque que la communion charnelle ne peut être sans l'acceptation du coeur, si minime soit-elle.

Si tu peux procréer sans aimer, rien que pour assouvir l'orgueil d'une mère déclinante, je te trouve vil. Dès lors, tu dégringoles de l'échelon supérieur, de la respectabilité où je t'ai toujours hissé. Ton raisonnement qui scinde est inadmissible: d'un côté, moi, "ta vie, ton amour, ton choix," de l'autre, "la petite Nabou, à supporter par devoir."

Mawdo, l'homme est un: grandeur et animalité confondues. Aucun geste de sa part n'est de pur idéal. Aucun geste de sa part n'est de pure bestialité.

Je me dépouille de ton amour, de ton nom. Vêtue du seul habit valable de la dignité, je poursuis ma route.

Adieu.

Aïssatou

(Mawdo,

Princes master their feelings to fulfil their duties. "Others" bend their heads and, in silence, accept a destiny that oppresses them.

That, briefly put, is the internal ordering of our society, with its absurd divisions. I will not yield to it. I cannot accept what you are offering me today in place of the happiness we once had. You want to draw a line between heartfelt love and physical love. I say that there can be no union of bodies without the heart's acceptance, however little that may be.

If you can procreate without loving, merely to satisfy the pride of your declining mother, then I find you despicable. At that moment you tumbled from the highest rung of respect on which I have always placed you. Your reasoning, which makes a distinction, is unacceptable to me: on one side, "your life, your love, your choice," on the other, "young Nabou, to be tolerated for reasons of duty."

Mawdo, man is one: greatness and animal fused together. None of his acts is pure charity. None is pure bestiality.

I am stripping myself of your love, your name. Clothed in my dignity, the only worthy garment, I go my way.) (50/31–32)

Aïssatou subsequently divorces Mawdo, moves into her own house, and goes back to school. Books, equalizers in a postcolonial patriarchal society, allow her to earn an advanced degree and an appointment in the Senegalese embassy in Washington, D.C., as an *interpreter*. Ramatoulaye and Aïssatou were among the first African females allowed access to literacy. They are situated, then, at the crossroads of orality and literature, which is embodied in Bâ's discourse.

Inscribing her own voice not only provides comfort for Ramatoulaye—she refers to her *cahier* (notebook) as a prop in a time of crisis—it also maintains and even solidifies her friendship with Aïssatou. This very long letter, in fact, resembles a diary in that it consists of daily entries in a notebook that is never sent to Aïssatou. The writing is prompted by the death of Ramatoulaye's husband of thirty years and her desire for closeness at this critical time in her life. It also allows her to reflect on her past and present situation. Ramatoulaye's initiation into writing as a tool of liberation, however, follows that of Aïssatou, who wrote a "lettre de rupture" to her husband Mawdo. While Ramatoulaye had verbally refused to marry Tamsir, her later rejection of Daouda Dieng's marriage proposal occurs in *written* form, for the following reasons. Although Ramatoulaye

respects Dieng, she does not love him, and he already has a wife. Ramatoulaye does not want to make another woman suffer as she did. At the
same time, however, Ramatoulaye does not completely abandon orality.
She sends Farmata, an old friend who is also a *griotte,* to deliver the letter
to Dieng personally at his place of work, a male's privileged space. In the
consulting room of his clinic, Dieng opens the sealed envelope and reads
while Farmata in turn maps the changing expression on his face. She becomes a silent witness to Ramatoulaye's rejection of someone she feels is an
ideal mate. Ramatoulaye has learned, perhaps from Aïssatou's example,
the power and permanence of inscribing women's voices in contemporary
society.

To female characters in the text, reading and writing are therapeutic,
liberating, empowering, authoritative. Books sustained Aïssatou during
her personal ordeal, while writing and reading her friend's letters, which
exhibit careful penmanship and emanate lavender perfume, sustain Ramatoulaye. On the other hand, male literacy is problematized in *Une si longue
lettre.* While he was in France studying law, Modou had written letters to
Ramatoulaye proclaiming his fidelity to her and lack of attraction to other
women, which would later prove to be false when he courts his daughter's
best friend while still married. Modou had also signed a document prom-
ising a monthly stipend to Dame Belle-mère, which was later overturned.
It is also while he is dictating a letter to a secretary that Modou has a heart
attack. Samba, Jacqueline's husband, is also haunted by his literacy. Love
letters and signed check stubs are tangible proof of his adultery. The young
can also be victims of their own literacy. Ramatoulaye's son Mawdo Fall,
who has a gift for writing, is the target of his philosophy teacher's racism.
His essays are graded very harshly, reflecting the teacher's reluctance to
allow a black student to be ranked first in the class. Writing for the males
in the text is thus disruptive, not comforting, and can lead to their undoing.

Ramatoulaye's very long letter to Aïssatou deconstructs the barrier
between oral and written discourse. The language and rhythm of the text
capture the cadences of the speaking voice: "Je souffle. J'ai raconté d'un
trait ton histoire et la mienne" (I take a deep breath. I've related at one go
your story as well as mine) (81/55). The narrator addresses her narratee
directly: sometimes by name—"Aïssatou," or "Aïssatou, mon amie"
(Aïssatou, my friend)—or simply as "mon amie" (my friend), "ma soeur"
(my sister), "ma meilleure amie" (my best friend). Most often she uses the
second person singular pronoun: "Toi, Aïssatou" (You, Aïssatou), "tu le
sais" (you know it), "Tu te rappelles" (you remember). Because the narratee, and by extension the reader, is inscribed in the text, a dialogue is
created.

Another characteristic of orality is found in the abundant use of proverbs and aphorisms in the text, especially by women. Tante Nabou advises Mawdo to accept her choice for his second wife in the following way: "la honte tue plus vite que la maladie" (Shame kills faster than disease) (48/ 30). Neighbors counsel Aïssatou to compromise and remain with Mawdo despite the fact that he has taken a young wife, using an adage: "On ne brûle pas un arbre qui porte des fruits" (You don't burn the tree which bears the fruit) (49/31). Ramatoulaye's grandmother transmits wisdom in the form of proverbs that explain the differences in children's personalities and how to cope with them.

Incomplete sentences can also imitate speech. With its short phrases, absence of verbs, and many exclamation points, the passage in which Ramatoulaye re-creates the moments surrounding Modou's death mimics the jerky, halting rhythm of someone who is agitated, out of breath: "Un taxi hélé! Vite! Plus vite! Ma gorge sèche. Dans ma poitrine une boule immobile. Vite! Plus vite! Enfin l'hôpital!" (A taxi quickly hailed! Fast! Fast! Faster still! My throat is dry. There is a rigid lump in my chest. Fast: faster still. At last, the hospital) (8/2). Oral syntax is also represented by the questions Ramatoulaye often asks herself: "Où me coucher?" (Where to lie down?) (9/2); "Partir? Recommencer à zéro, après avoir vécu vingt-cinq ans avec un homme, après avoir mis au monde douze enfants?" (Leave? Start again at zero, after living twenty-five years with one man, after having borne twelve children?) (60/39). Advice is usually given in the form of a maxim. Ramatoulaye, like Télumée, reinserts women into the oral tradition.

Women's voices from all ages and social classes prevail in *Une si longue lettre:* from aristocratic Tante Nabou, who provides instruction to her niece Petite Nabou orally, to *griotte* Farmata who verbalizes and articulates for the first time the pregnancy of an unmarried daughter of Ramatoulaye; from Ramatoulaye's grandmother, who is represented by her aphorisms to Daba, who intervenes on behalf of her younger brother, talking to his prejudiced teacher. While Ramatoulaye is never reticent about communicating with her best friend, Aïssatou, despite their class differences, she is discrete in other circumstances. Her criticism of mourners who pay a condolence call just for the food, for example, is not expressed out loud, but is confined to her letter. After her confrontation with Tamsir, however, she becomes more outspoken, engaging in a serious discussion with Daouda Dieng on the indispensability of women representatives in the legislature. The women's voices inscribed in Ramatoulaye's diary, except for the mourners, are not engaged in gossip, as women's voices are often represented, but are powerful agents.

Women's solidarity, so important in "Nguessi Ngonda" and *Une si longue lettre,* also frames Michèle Maillet's *L'étoile noire* (Black star) (1990). The protagonist's circumstances—confinement in a Nazi concentration camp—encourage competition for food and clothing, but survival depends on cooperation. Sidonie Hellénon defies complete isolation by forming bonds with some of her *codétenues* (co-detainees) and secretly recording her experiences in a notebook for posterity. These relationships which are not longstanding like Ramatoulaye's and Aïssatou's are born out of crisis and cross racial boundaries.

Although Sidonie Hellénon, a twenty-five-year-old mother of two, Martinican and Catholic, is separated by race and religion from most of the other people on the train to the concentration camp, she yearns to establish a connection to someone. According to Ronald Sharp, "one of the crucial stages in the formation of most friendships is the long conversation in which one shares one's past with one's emerging friend" (16). Sidonie, noticing Suzanne, a young French woman about her age, is discouraged from initiating a conversation, realizing that time is a luxury she does not have: "alors pourquoi se lier si vite et pour si peu de temps?" (Why forge a bond so quickly and for such a short amount of time?) (51). It is Suzanne who establishes contact, using her body to communicate. By making a path for Sidonie and her young children as they disembark from the train, protecting them during the bumpy bus ride, holding Désiré's hand, and consoling a crying Nicaise, Suzanne demonstrates to Sidonie her willingness to invest in a relationship. Although Sidonie and Suzanne do not speak, a friendship blossoms. Sharp's "long conversation" has been replaced in this context by Sidonie's voice, which is inscribed on her body language.

This silent but articulate discourse takes many forms in the narrative: a nod, a smile, a look, a movement of the eyelid, a hand gesture, a hand touching the shoulder, a nudge, an extended arm. These silent signals have meaning and, more often than not, replace speech: "J'effleure la joue de Suzanne, qui ouvre les yeux dans un sourire. Elle suit mon regard, mon geste. Elle a compris" (I touch Suzanne's cheek. She opens her eyes in a smile. She follows my gaze, my gesture. She understood) (78). Sometimes Sidonie and Suzanne need not even look at one another: "Nous n'échangeons plus un mot, plus un regard, mais je sens que nous sommes désormais quatre, deux enfants, deux femmes, une petite communauté dans la foule, un peu plus qu'une famille" (We do not exchange words or glances any more, but I feel that we are henceforth four, two children, two women, a small community in the crowd, a little more than a family) (56). Sidonie eventually characterizes their relationship as a friendship, but one that must be hidden at all costs:

> Mais Suzanne est devenue mon double, et moi le sien. Nous sommes comme Désiré et Nicaise, jumelles. Nous ne communiquons pas par mots, mais par signes, et le plus souvent par notre simple présence. Nous craignons la jalousie, l'envie des autres. L'amitié est une denrée rare; on ne peut pas la voler, mais on peut la détruire.

> (But Suzanne became my double, and I hers. We are like Désiré and Nicaise, twins. We do not communicate with words, but with signs, and most often with our mere presence. We fear the jealousy and envy of others. Friendship is a rare commodity; it cannot be stolen, but it can be destroyed.) (180)[2]

In *L'étoile noire* not only does Sidonie form an alliance with Suzanne, but also with women of color: Carol, a black singer from the United States; Anastasie, a Martinican and daughter of Sidonie's former teacher; Algaé, a Senegalese housekeeper for a family of *résistants;* Eloise, a Malagasy; and Nadine, a Chinese. Their common bond, a "solidarité de couleur" (solidarity of color) (198) is responsible for their separation from the other women and subjection to particular scientific experiments by the Nazis. In order to cope under such horrible conditions, they try to calm and comfort one another. Carol, the African American, teaches the others spirituals; Anastasie helps deliver an unnamed black woman's baby. Sometimes they rely on silent discourse to communicate: Eloise questions Sidonie with a look; Sidonie, in turns, reads her eyes.

Sidonie and Anastasie, who are compatriots, become especially close. Sidonie cares for her when she has a fever. While in different cells, they sing Creole songs to each other and cry in silence and sing a newly learned spiritual when Carol dies from harsh punishment for resisting. Sidonie refers to Anastasie as not only her friend, but her memory. Perhaps the most convincing sign of their friendship is that when Sidonie learns that she will be transferred to yet another camp and certain death, she entrusts to Anastasie her three most precious possessions for safekeeping: her medallion given to her by her mother; her son Désiré, if he is found; and her journal, in the hope that it will be read by someone after her death as a testimony to her suffering. Close bonds among women are essential to their survival.

In regrouping these women of color from Africa, the Caribbean, and the United States in war-torn Europe of 1943, Maillet not only makes a strong statement about origins and diasporic reconnections, she revisits the Middle Passage and slavery as well. When Sidonie is being moved to another camp, a memory is triggered, transporting her back in time. The stifling freight train in which she is riding is transformed into a slave ship and she detects the noise of the ocean. The Middle Passage is re-created in her mind as the sighs of her fellow passengers become

> un autre chant, une autre plainte, un écho de ma conscience, une houle douloureuse et sonore qui s'enfle et fait battre mon sang et mon pouls comme un sanglot. Est-ce celle qu'entendaient ceux qu'on appelait 'le bois d'ébène' dans les fonds de cale des vieux voiliers qui les transportaient vers les Amériques?

> (another song, another moan, an echo of my conscience, a doleful and sonorous swell that rises and makes my blood and pulse beat like a sob. Is it the one that those that were called ebony wood heard in the holds of the old sailing ships that brought them to the Americas?) (83)

Dispersed by the slave trade and relocated to the Americas, these women are again brought together in a crisis in Europe. Sidonie's deportation, separation from her five-year-old twins, tattooing, forced labor, and physical and emotional violence lead her to contemplate the parallels with slavery: "Cet esclavage, je le connais. Les gares du désespoir aujourd'hui, les ports de l'angoisse hier: je me sens chargée des mêmes chaines" (I know this slavery. The stations of hopelessness today, the ports of anguish yesterday, I feel loaded down with the same chains) (87–88).[3] She concludes: "Trois siècles après mes ancêtres, me voilà donc bien revenue au point de départ: l'esclavage" (three centuries after my ancestors, here I am back at the point of departure: slavery) (118). One especially cruel guard remarks that the Germans are completing the "civilizing mission" that the English, Dutch, French, Spanish, and Portuguese had begun centuries earlier. Sidonie draws strength from her ancestors who rebelled, and entertains the idea of holding secret strategy meetings in the camp. Her awakening consciousness to history is a kind of rebirth. That Sidonie was born during the Christmas season and also arrested in December reinforces that idea.

By the nature of her ordeal, Sidonie gives voice to captive Africans, especially women, on their way to the Americas. She does not, however, trust her experiences to the memory of others. After all, the oral and written traces of slavery had been erased by the ancestors of the perpetrators as well as those of the victims. Not only were the horrors of slavery omitted from the official French historical records, her parents had "répété, affirmé que l'esclavage était oublié, envolé, aboli. Ils allaient presque jusqu'à faire comme si cela n'avait jamais existé" (repeated, affirmed that slavery was forgotten, disappeared, abolished. They went almost as far as acting as if it had never existed) (26–27). In the face of this collective amnesia, which Michel de Certeau posits is not a passive process, but "an action directed against the past" (3–4), Sidonie takes pains to write everything down, keeping a journal ("Pour l'instant ma mémoire est dans ce carnet" [for the moment my memory is in this notebook]) (190), in the hope that it will be read by someone after her death as a testimony to her suffering. Her jailers, however, aware of the power of the written word, forbid writing, so Sidonie makes entries in her diary in secret, drawing on her background as a writer of children's stories. Her present situation, however, requires that she strive for a broader audience. Since her capture, she has just taken brief notes. It is during her six-month confinement at Ravensbruck that she comes to realize the importance of chronicling her experiences for posterity. Starting from the last page of the imitation leather notebook (*carnet*, the same color as her ancestor Agénor's skin) and marking the place and day, she proceeds to record everything from that day on. At the same time she goes back to the beginning of the notebook to fill in the gaps before she forgets; in other words, reconstructing the past. She literally writes forward and backward, knowing that they will intersect one day, in the middle of the notebook. Consequently, this *double écriture* (double writing) records not only her story but also represents that of her African ancestors who were also captured, relocated, and enslaved, but whose story was silenced and erased from official records. By implication, Sidonie's notebook functions as another archive, providing previously undocumented evidence on the Middle Passage, slavery, as well as the Holocaust. Maillet herself was inspired to write the novel after she learned through extensive research that more than two thousand black women had died in Nazi death camps (Lequeret 17).

One obstacle to this inscription is that as a prisoner Sidonie has no right to personal possessions. Her rudimentary materials are a stubby pencil, which subjects her writing to erasure, and a small notebook. The recording of her voice, then, is hampered, restricted: "mon trésor de papier diminue . . . Et j'ai tant à dire" (my treasured supply of paper is diminishing . . . and I have so much to say) (186). Sidonie rises to the challenge, but the notebook must be hidden from the guards: in a wall, under a floor plank, or in her apron while she takes a shower. As she loses strength from fatigue and tuberculosis, writing becomes more and more difficult and she stops dating the entries. The notebook is transformed into a site of testimony, of resistance:

Il faut que quelqu'un sache où j'ai laissé ma vie, mon âme. A quoi bon toutes ces ruses, toute cette énergie dépensée si mon carnet doit rester à jamais sous cette planche, si le temps seul lit ma souffrance, et efface et gomme peu à peu les griffes si fragiles du crayon sur le papier?

(Someone has to know where I left my life, my soul. What good are all these ruses, all of this energy spent if my notebook should remain forever under this plank, if only time reads my suffering, and erases little by little the fragile pencil scratches on paper?) (180–81)

To that end, before being transferred to Mauthausen, Sidonie entrusts the notebook to Anastasie for safekeeping:

Si tu survis, dis à tous ce que nous avons vécu ici. Sauve le petit carnet où j'ai pris des notes. Tu sais où il est caché. J'y ai écrit tout ce que j'ai vu, tout ce que j'ai enduré depuis mon arrestation. Avant de quitter ce lieu d'enfer pour toujours, je vais remplir la dernière page blanche qui me reste.

(If you survive, tell everyone what we experienced here. Save the little notebook in which I took notes. You know where it is hidden. In it I wrote all that I saw, all that I endured since my arrest. Before leaving this hell-hole forever, I will fill up the last blank page I have left.) (244)

The inscription of Sidonie's story is reminiscent of a slave narrative or a Holocaust diary, both of which emphasize personal testimony. They are also exemplary texts in that they are representative of other lives. Sidonie's inscribed voice speaks for others, "notre vie ici," she writes." "Pour que l'on y croit, pour que l'on n'oublie pas" (so that one believes what happened here, so that no one will forget) (186); "Nous ne pouvons disparaître tout à fait de la surface de la terre: nos noms sont inscrits là, sur ce registre, à tout jamais" (We cannot completely disappear from the face of the earth; our names are inscribed on this register, forever) (121).

Despite its emphasis on writing, *L'étoile noire* contains several narrative strategies that recall speech. The exclamations, repetitions, and direct address to her ancestor Agénor suggest a grounding in the women's storytelling tradition. At the same time, however, Sidonie inscribes her voice onto the written page, inserting her text into the written tradition.

Bâ and Maillet's inscription of women's friendship contrasts sharply with the representations in orature I examined in chapter 1. It is useful to briefly revisit some of those constructions here. Typical sayings from Congo and Cameroon, respectively, are: "The banana tree is felled by the wind; friendship is felled by a married woman"; "If friendship includes the wife, it will perish" (Schipper 80). A similar message is found in Birago Diop's "Les mamelles" (The humps). According to the narrator, two wives in the same household will always be rivals:

> Lorsqu'il s'agit d'épouses, deux n'est point un bon compte. Pour qui veut s'éviter souvent querelles, cris, reproches et allusions malveillantes, il faut trois femmes ou une seule et non pas deux. Deux femmes dans une même maison ont toujours avec elles une troisième compagne qui non seulement n'est bonne à rien, mais encore se trouve être la pire des mauvaises conseillères. Cette compagne c'est l'Envie à la voix aigre et acide comme du jus de tamarin.

> (In the matter of wives two is not a good number. The man who wants to avoid quarrels, shouting, grousing, reproaches, and nasty innuendos must have at least three wives, or else one, but never two. Two women in the same house always have with them a third companion, who is not only good for nothing, but also happens to be the worst of bad counsellors. This companion is shrill-voiced Envy, bitter as tamarind juice.) (33/2)

The two wives in question are Khary, the jealous, selfish first wife, and Koumba, the amiable, generous second wife. Koumba shares information with Khary that will make her hunchback disappear, but Khary abuses that trust. "N'Gor Niébé" also from *Les contes d'Amadou Koumba* illustrates the differences between male and female friendship. N'Gor has never revealed to his male friends why he does not eat string beans. On the other hand, N'Dèné's friends always share confidences. In fact, the reason N'Gor gives for not explaining his dietary choices to Dèné is precisely that she will tell her best friend, Thioro, who will tell her best friend, N'Goné, who will tell her best friend, Djégane. Female friendship manifested through talk is represented in this *conte* not as a mutually supportive location, but as a threat to men.

In Haitian orature female friendship is also discredited. It is established at the outset of the story "Séraphine et Lilas," in *Contes et légendes d'Haïti,* that the title characters' friendship is rare because two beautiful women are usually rivals. Their secret is that they enjoy doing different things; Séraphine reads and sews, Lilas prefers an active social life. The depth of their friendship is manifested when Lilas contracts leprosy and Séraphine offers to let her borrow her skin to go dancing. Lilas, however, runs off and marries her favorite partner, leaving Séraphine with the unsightly skin. When Séraphine finally locates Lilas and demands her skin back, Lilas's husband, repelled by her appearance, abandons her. In addition to illustrating the importance of physical beauty in attracting and keeping a husband, it also very clearly indicates that women who are friends will eventually betray one another. Again, like in "N'Gor Niébé," communication among women is stigmatized and leads to their downfall.[4] In orature female friendships are rarely represented, but in women's texts rivalry does not always characterize women's relationships.

Ousmane Sembène creates women characters who resemble more closely the women found in women-centered/woman-narrated texts in that cooperation rather than rivalry characterizes most of the relationships in *Les bouts de bois de Dieu* (1960). Not only do the women form alliances to support their striking railway worker husbands, but they make their own statement by marching from Thiès to Dakar and successfully routing the police. While they collaborate for a political cause, they also relate to one another on a more personal basis. The families survive the hardships due, in large part, to the women's efforts to help one another. In addition, Penda, who had been ostracized because of her unorthodox lifestyle, not only wins the respect of the community because of her commitment, but she also earns the friendship of Maïmouna. In this narrative, even friendship between males and females is possible, although doomed. Bakayoko tells N'Dèye Touti that Penda "c'était une vraie amie et elle a donné sa vie" (was a real friend, and she lost her life because of it) (342/303). Sembène also shows that there can be tragic consequences when women friends lack close contact—verbal or physical—in a time of crisis. In "La noire de . . ." (The Promised Land), Diouana, from rural Casamance, leaves Senegal to be a maid in the south of France. Separated from her family and friends she is dependent on Madame, her employer, to write letters home. Also separated from Madame by race, class, and language, she is unable to confide in her. Diouana feels powerless, both verbally and financially:

> Etait-ce possible de dire tout ce qui lui passait par la tête à Madame? Elle s'en voulait. Son ignorance la rendait muette. Elle écumait de rage, à son propos. Mademoiselle lui avait, en plus, pris les timbres.

> But was it possible to say to Madame all that went through her mind? She was angry with herself, for her ignorance silenced her. This impotence on her part made her foam with rage. Moreover, Mademoiselle had taken her stamps. (182/98)

Isolated, alienated, reduced to silence—in short, unable to communicate orally or in writing—Diouana commits suicide.

Diouana's situation is figured otherwise in Ousmane Sembène's short story in the same collection, "Lettres de France" (1962), in which Nafi, in her coffinlike attic room in Marseilles, writes letters to her unnamed friend in Dakar. The nature of this relationship is clearly identified: "Avec toi, je remue le fond de mon âme. Tu es une âme. Une vraie Chose rare" (With you I can pour my heart out. You're my real friend) (82/59). Nafi discloses her disillusionment with her life in France and her regret and disappointment for having married poor seventy-three-year-old Demba. Silence characterizes her marriage, while open communication characterizes the friendship. For example, when Nafi becomes pregnant, she confides in her friend even before she tells her husband or other family members. Nafi recognizes that friendship sustained through writing has been her salvation:

> Que serais-je devenue sans toi? Toi, mon unique soutien, ma confidente! Tu ne sauras et ne pourras jamais savoir comment j'ai apprécié notre correspondance. Sans ce flux et reflux de lettres, j'aurais été sevrée de mon lait originel, une perdue, une égarée. Je ne suis pas une lyrique, mais, je voudrais pouvoir t'écrire pour te faire sentir toutes mes émotions. Nos tête-à-tête—malgré cette quantité d'eau qui nous sépare—furent pour moi, les joints qui solidifient notre amitié.

> (What would have happened to me if it weren't for you? My one support, the only person I could confide in. You'll never know just how much our correspondence has meant to me. Without this coming and going of letters, I should have been cut off from my source, been lost, and gone astray. I'm not a poet, but I wish I could write and make you feel all my emotions. Despite all the water between us, our exchanges have put the seal on our friendship.) (114/76)

Nafi's elegy to friendship is mirrored and expanded in and even prefigures Ramatoulaye and Sidonie's texts.

The *cahiers/carnets* that Ramatoulaye and Sidonie compose in *Une si longue lettre* and *L'étoile noire*, respectively, not only inscribe women's voices but are also meant to be read by others. In other words, these female authors—Bâ and Maillet—who inscribe women's voices inscribing themselves—Ramatoulaye and Sidonie—transform their narrators into authors. This "double auteur(ité)" subverts hegemonic discourses in that it not only valorizes women's experiences but, because it is addressed to someone else, it also represents knowledge passed on, like female storytellers' wisdom. Diaries and letters with a difference—that is, those that are not private documents—are prevalent in narratives by francophone African and Caribbean women writers. Michèle Lacrosil's *Sapotille et le serin d'argile* (1960) is the diary of a young Guadeloupean who relives childhood and adolescence while crossing the Atlantic. Jacqueline Manicom's *La Graine: Journal d'une sage-femme* is in the form of a journal. Mariotte fills up seven notebooks in André and Simone Schwarz-Bart's *Un plat de porc aux bananes vertes* (1967). In Myriam Warner-Vieyra's *Juletane*, the title character's journal is intended for her husband, who unfortunately dies before its completion. Nonetheless, it is read by Hélène Parpin, who discovers it in a folder. Juletane chose an almost empty *cahier* that she appropriated from her co-wife's oldest daughter. The *cahier* metonymically replaces the child Juletane never had. At one point she hides it under her dress, tying it to her waist. She is not purposely simulating pregnancy, but the reader can make the connection between her producing a child and producing a written text. Writing in the journal assumes an important function, as in *Une si longue lettre* and *L'étoile noire*, the therapeutic value of which cannot be underestimated: it replaces speech ("Je suis restée si longtemps silencieuse" (I remained silent so long) (94); it becomes a friend, a confidant, and witness; and finally, the memories it resuscitates allow Juletane to analyze, endure, and resist life's pain. Maméga's account of a Martinican domestic's life in France fills up several notebooks in Françoise Ega's *Lettres à une noire*. The narrative is equally a woman's struggle to be taken seriously as a writer despite discouraging words from her husband and interference from her children. Maméga, realizing this difficult struggle is not unique, decides not to send the *cahiers* to her Brazilian counterpart/destinataire, Carolina, because it is a story she already knows (3, 213).

Women writers, like their characters, have also expressed the need to be heard, through writing. According to Haitian novelist Marie-Thérèse Colimon: "Je suis née avec le goût d'écrire" (quoted in Condé, *La Parole*, 117). Senegalese poet Ndèye Coumba Mbengue Diakhaté uses writing to express her innermost thoughts: "Je me suis trouvée dans les conditions telles que j'éprouvais le besoin de m'exprimer, de parler, de me confier. Une pudeur me retient de me confier à quelqu'un. Je me suis confiée aux papiers" (I found myself under conditions in which I felt the need to express myself, to speak, to confide. Modesty keeps me from confiding in someone. I confided in my papers) ("Entretien" 37). Ken Bugul expressed a similar desire to confide in someone: "Je ne pouvais me confier à personne alors j'ai mis tout cela sur du papier" (I could not confide in anyone, so I put everything down on paper) (Magnier 152). In other words, these women seek an outlet for their voices through writing. One safe space they find is the blank page. The cover of the first edition of *Une si longue lettre,* which pictures the arm of a black woman, pen in hand, in the act of writing, is thus emblematic of the woman's voice long stifled that is finally heard—through writing.

Cooperation and friendship are privileged in the literature of women from French-speaking Africa and the Caribbean. Aminata Maïga Kâ's short story "Le miroir de la vie" encapsulates what I discussed in this chapter. It closes with a letter from Adji Arame Dieng to her friend Adji Aminta Ndiaye, whose consoling function reproduces that of the correspondence between Rama and Aïssatou. That Adji Arame's maid, Fatou, confides only in Adji Arame's daughter Ndeye illustrates a level of friendship that crosses class lines. In *Une si longue lettre* and *L'étoile noire,* bonding and confiding—in one word, friendship—structure the text. Whether communication takes place orally, in writing, or by gesture is immaterial, it is essential to the survival of women in that it provides emotional support, especially in difficult circumstances.

5

Muffled Voices Break Free

Calixthe Beyala's *C'est le soleil qui m'a brûlée* and Marie Vieux Chauvet's *Amour*

Ils m'empêchent d'ouvrir la bouche pour exprimer mes idées alors qu'elles m'étouffent.

(They prevent me from opening my mouth in order to express my ideas when they [my ideas] stifle me.)

—Marie Chauvet, *Amour, colère et folie*

Je hurlais et ce hurlement, tel celui d'un nouveau-né terrifié, salua mon retour dans le monde . . . Je dus réapprendre à parler, à communiquer avec mes semblables, à ne plus me contenter de rares monosyllabes.

(I screamed, and this scream, the terrified cry of a newborn baby, heralded my return to this world . . . I had to learn how to speak again, how to communicate with my fellow creatures, and no longer be content with a word here and there.)

Maryse Condé, *Moi, Tituba sorcière . . . noire de Salem*

Muffled voices could refer to Ramatoulaye or Sidonie in *Une si longue lettre* and *L'étoile noire*, respectively, as both narrators struggle to be heard through writing; however, in this chapter, they designate nineteen-year-old Ateba Léocadie in Calixthe Beyala's *C'est le soleil qui m'a brûlée* (1987), who, like Ramatoulaye, writes letters to achieve voice, and Claire Clamont in Marie Vieux Chauvet's *Amour* (1968), who, like Sidonie, keeps a diary to counter voicelessness and invisibility. I explore how these powerless, fragmented, and exploited protagonists, virtual prisoners of society, undergo a major transformation, rebel against oppression with an act of violence, and advance toward subjectivity. According to Frantz Fanon, killing the oppressor is not in itself liberating, a fact that renders Ateba's and Claire's final act, though heroic, nonetheless, ambiguous. These narratives carefully inscribe women's voices who have virtually no access to speech.

Although Cameroonian Beyala and Haitian Chauvet represent different generations, they share the distinction of having resided abroad and being controversial figures. All seven of Beyala's novels were published in France, where she lives. Since *Le petit prince de Belleville* was published in 1992, she has faced charges of plagiarism.[1] Additionally, Beyala has been the target of criticism by many African women who greeted *Lettre d'une africaine à ses soeurs occidentales* (1995) with hostility due to its subject and tone. Some felt that Beyala made erroneous and sweeping generalizations about African women, reducing their condition to the issue of excision. Marie Chauvet's residence abroad was, in effect, an exile precipitated by the publication of the politically charged *Amour, colère et folie* in 1968, which angered the Duvalier regime to the point where her husband's family purchased all of the available copies. No stranger to controversy before she fled to New York, Chauvet had been criticized in certain circles for performing in her own plays. Being an actress was not considered the "proper" profession for a member of her class, according to her daughter Erma Saint-Grégoire.

While "Nguessi Ngonda," with its themes and inscription of women's voices prefigures *Pluie et vent sur Télumée Miracle, Une si longue lettre,* and *L'étoile noire,* the Bassa women's oral story is subverted in *Amour* and *C'est le soleil qui m'a brûlée.*[2] Nguessi Ngonda attains her ultimate goal— marriage—through her own initiative, power, and alliances with other women, but Ateba and Claire fail to articulate their goals and lack a female support system. Furthermore, the main male characters in *C'est le soleil qui m'a brûlée* and *Amour* are not acquiescent like Johnny Waka, but overly aggressive to the point of being violent. Nonetheless, Ateba and Claire are at once attracted and repulsed by them.

The novel's title, *C'est le soleil qui m'a brûlée,* inscribes women's orality in that it designates a female voice offering an explanation for her dark skin. The title is actually borrowed from the first poem from the Bible's Song of Songs, a dialogue celebrating erotic love. The novel's epigraph offers more of the poem, in which a girl, whose punishment by her brothers is banishment to the vineyards, pleads with the daughters of Jerusalem not to fear her dark skin—it is the sun that is responsible for her color. The stigma of race/color/gender, the separation from one's family, and the resulting lack of protection resonate in *C'est le soleil qui m'a brûlée,* although explicit references to the biblical excerpt do not occur in the text.[3] Nineteen-year-old protagonist Ateba Léocadie embodies the young woman in the biblical poem. Abandoned by her prostitute mother, Ateba articulates displacement and seeks connections with other women.

C'est le soleil qui m'a brûlée reterritorializes the poem from Song of Songs from its rural setting to a postindependence urban Cameroon. The neighborhood, called QG, for "quartier général," and situated at the end of Liberty Boulevard, is one in which rats, flies, garbage, oppressive heat, poverty, and prostitution proliferate, an area so dangerous that taxi drivers are reluctant to take passengers there. The guidance, nurturing, and protection traditionally provided by women to girls is lacking in that environment. There is no dialogue between Ateba and her guardian, Aunt Ada, no comforting words of advice, no aphorisms from the older generation like we saw between Reine Sans Nom and Télumée in *Pluie et vent sur Télumée Miracle* or *Une si longue lettre,* just shouted orders reminding Ateba to complete her chores. In fact, Ateba's circumstances resemble somewhat those of Télumée; both are raised by an "other mother" when their own mothers abandon them for a lover. But for Ateba, there is no Reine Sans Nom to fill that void. Despite Ateba's desire for a confidante and dialogue, she is forced to endure alone: "elle décide de monologuer" (she decides to talk to herself) (26/10) because Aunt Ada and neighbor Combi are inadequate surrogates. Ateba's relationship with her contemporary Irène comes closest to a traditional female friendship in that they share confidences, but the level of support and reciprocity in no way approximates Ramatoulaye and Aïssatou's relationship in *Une si longue lettre* or even Sidonie and Suzanne and Anastasie's experience in *L'étoile noire.* Ateba does accompany Irène to the hospital when she has an abortion, but Irène does not offer similar support to Ateba in her time of need. Competition, rather, is a part of their relationship. When Irène shares information about her sexual escapades, Ateba is expected to come up with a better story, to outdo her. Ateba questions this new order in which women's solidarity is no longer the norm.

The conditions in the "quartier général" do not afford young women the opportunity to express themselves. In Beyala's text, men, in particular, are obstacles to women's speech. For example, Ateba is rendered mute in front of Jean Zepp, a roomer in Ada's house: "chaque fois qu'ils se sont croisés, les sons l'ont désertée, les mots sont restés collés à ses lèvres" (every time they crossed each other's path, sound abandoned her, words remained glued to her lips) (37/19). Speech, however, was not always foreign to Ateba. She used to enjoy engaging in pseudo-philosophical discussions with her schoolmates. Since leaving the *lycée,* however, she has exchanged that particular mode of communication for other discourses—self-recitation and letter writing—confiding her thoughts to herself, to God, or to paper. In fact, Ateba's voice is muffled to the point where she does not relate her own story; it is filtered through the narrator, Moi.[4]

Moi can be construed as the narrator/storyteller/*conteuse* in *C'est le soleil qui m'a brûlée*. It is her voice that opens the novel. Quotation marks and italics, graphic signs of orality, separate Moi's voice from the text proper. An invisible female spirit and the primary narrator, she identifies herself as Ateba's soul. She claims to understand Ateba's distress and vows to help her to the best of her ability. Subverting silence, she does not hesitate to locate the source of her anger: "J'ai envie de parler . . . J'ai terriblement envie de parler de cette aube triste, de ces heures qui ont couru avant l'arrivée de l'homme. . . . Je puis dire sans attenter à la vérité que c'est sa faute" (I feel like talking . . . I have a terrible urge to talk about that sad dawn, about those hours that fled by before the arrival of man. . . . Without doing violence to the truth, I can say that it is his fault) (13/2). This is the first allusion to the tale about women's generosity, sacrifice, and subsequent betrayal that Ateba will recount at Irène's funeral.

This episode can be viewed not only as women's attempt to reclaim voice, but it also demonstrates the community's abandonment of its ancestral oral tradition. Although Ateba is an adept storyteller—words pour out of her: "elle devient un torrent de mots" (she becomes a torrent of words) (168/115), those in attendance at Irène's funeral do not wish to hear the story about women's origins on earth, when women were shining stars in the sky and responded to the pleas of lonely men on earth. After abandoning their home and bringing the men light and love—their mission accomplished—the women wish to return home. The men repay, or rather betray, their benefactors by stealing their containers of light and surrounding their house with an iron thread. The former rescuers, now prisoners, weep, and their copious tears form the earth's lakes, rivers, and seas. This story of women's disempowerment indeed revises "Nguessi Ngonda." The solution to the dilemma, that women unite in order to regain their rightful place in the world, is obvious to Ateba, who muses wistfully: "Pourquoi les étoiles qui déchirent le ciel ne s'unissent-elles pas au soleil?" (But why do the stars that pierce the sky not unite with the sun?) (64/39).

Unfortunately, Ateba's impatient audience at the funeral dismisses her. Although this performance occurs late in the novel, there are numerous allusions to this story of betrayal throughout the text. One such example is when Jean Zepp convinces Ada to rent him a room in her house—the one that offers the most light. Symbolically, it represents the male who usurps the female's power. The tale of the men imprisoning women on earth created by Beyala intersects with Christian doctrine as the story complements the biblical poem Song of Songs.

The female body in *C'est le soleil* is invested with meaning. Objectified, degraded, exploited, and abused, it is, as a result, nonproductive, which is anathema in African cultures. Betty's stomach is dried up like an old date; childless Ada's teeth resemble the ironwork of a sewer; wrinkled old women resemble rusted cans. The reader can chart prostitution and rape, two perversions of sexuality in the narrative that function as tropes of the condition of certain poor women in a postcolonial African inner city. Studies on prostitution in Africa reveal that it was brought on by the breakdown of traditional family structures due to colonization and urbanization. According to Paulette Songue, it is one of the few ways women can earn a living in a city.[5] Ateba, who follows in her mother, Betty's, footsteps, Ekassi, and Irène are neither heroic nor martyred like Penda in Sembène's *Les bouts de bois de Dieu*. Ekassi turns to prostitution after being abandoned by her lover, recently released from jail. Irène dies after an abortion. In desperation, Ateba then picks up a client in a bar, who calls her a whore. Prostitution, however, is not gender restricted. The scene in which Jean Zepp negotiates the price of a room could be read as a transaction between a client and prostitute. In renting him the *chambre lumière*, the one with the most light, which is associated with women in the story Ateba will relate, Ada plays the role of the pimp, allowing him access to a previously female space.

Male characters in Beyala's text are responsible, in part, for the abuse of women's bodies. They are routinely possessive, destructive, and irresponsible—in one word, dangerous. Ada's first husband, Samba, died from alcoholism, and her current live-in companion, Yossep, beats her. Ekassi's former lover was a thief. Betty routinely suffers beatings at the hands of her lover. Ateba's body is particularly vulnerable. Jean Zepp insults her, shakes her, and grips her hair. A soldier throws her to the ground, demands sexual favors when he asks to see her identity papers. Even the benign celebration marking the seventh day after Ekassi's death is a site of male vulgarity. The mere touch by a potential dance partner renders Ateba a prisoner: "La main la rattrape, possessive, encombrante, sourde aux réactions de son corps, au dégoût qu'elle jette dans ses reins" (the hand grabs her again, possessively, bearing down, deaf to her body's reactions, to the disgust that it pours into her insides) (138–39/94). The anonymous customer Ateba picks up after Irène's funeral claims her body as his property: "ton corps m'appartient jusqu'à l'aube" (your body belongs to me until dawn) (172/118). When he objects to her leaving his apartment, he grasps her wrists and hair, forcing her to kneel and perform oral sex. This display of physical power complements his assertion that that position is God's natural place for women. It is after this assault that Ateba reacts with violence. Hitting him with a copper ashtray, banging his head against the floor, stabbing him with a knife, is her way of exacting revenge in the name of Irène and other women, since their arrival on earth.

In *C'est le soleil qui m'a brûlée* female characters are sometimes accomplices in the manipulation of bodies. Beyala clearly denounces the custom in which a specialist inserts an egg into Ateba's vagina to verify her virginity. This practice is Ada's way of controlling her niece's sexuality. When the test proves that Ateba's hymen is intact, the women celebrate the occasion; but for Ateba it is a painful and humiliating experience. Through masturbation she seeks to reclaim her body. Beyala also problematizes circumcision in a scene where women cheer at an initiation ceremony. Upon seeing the bleeding penis, Ateba experiences a *plaisir trouble* (uneasy pleasure) (42/22). The oxymoron prefigures her later stabbing a client after he rapes her. Ateba's friend Irène, whose body is procured by her clients, escapes their touch by turning off her feelings.

While the mother's body is honored for its reproductive capabilities in African and Caribbean cultures, mothers are absent or motherhood is represented as traumatic in *C'est le soleil qui m'a brûlée*. During the ceremony cited above, the initiate calls out for his mother's help, but to no avail. Betty and Irène's pregnant bodies are devoured by the fetus. Ateba's grandmother could not prevent the premature deaths of nine of her eleven children; only Ada and Betty survived. Ada, who has no children of her own, fails in her role as "other mother" to Ateba and asserts that motherhood is a burden. Irène, whose mother is senile, dies after an abortion.

Most important to examine is the relationship between Ateba and her mother, Betty, which collapsed early, the roles reversed. It was a young Ateba who waited for Betty to return home late each night from walking the streets, and who massaged her tired body. Ateba spends her life trying to imagine her mother after she leaves for good, using photographs found in a trunk to reconstruct the past. The women characters in *C'est le soleil* do not leave any heirs. The failed mothers in *C'est le soleil* are powerless like their ancestors in the legend.

The universe in *C'est le soleil* is upside down. Ateba searches for an escape from this environment by retreating alone to her room, where she reads and imagines herself as the heroine of a novel. She writes letters to God and to imaginary women, telling them to be ready so as not to miss the arrival of the stars, this time to rescue *women,* thereby revising the ending to the tale about humans' origins on earth. She can confide only in them individually:

A toi seule, je peux dire certaines choses, n'être plus moi, me fondre
en toi, car je te les dis mieux à toi qu'à moi-même. J'aime à t'imaginer
à mes côtés, guidant mes pas et mes rêves, mes désirs enfouis dans le
désert de ce monde incohérent.

(To you alone can I say certain things; I don't have to be me anymore,
I can melt away in you, for I say them better to you than to myself.
I love imagining you by my side, guiding my steps and my dreams, my
desires buried deep inside the desert of this incoherent world.) (67/
41)

But Ateba's confidence in writing wanes. On the one hand, she burns or
makes paper airplanes out of the letters she composes. On the other hand,
on a broader scale, despite her writing skills, there is no indication in the
text that Ateba has a regular job. Although she is trapped in a milieu that
offers no outlet for her literacy, she realizes the importance of the relationship between reading and writing: "Elle prétend que lire permet d'imaginer
des histoires à écrire. Elle dit souvent qu'un jour elle deviendra écrivain"
(She claims that reading leads to imagining stories to be written. She often
says that one day she will become a writer) (64/39). It is in part male
dominance that interferes with Ateba's dreams of becoming a writer. Jean
interrupts her while she is reading, announcing his desire for them to become friends. When his "proposition" is met with silence, he resorts to
buying her companionship (a form of prostitution) by putting a five hundred CFA bill between her breasts and dictating where and when they will
meet the next day.

The issue of women's voice surfaces again at the close of the novel as
Moi, witnessing Ateba killing the client who raped her, addresses the
reader: "Moi qui vous raconte cette histoire" (I who am telling you this
story) (173/118); "Mais Moi, Moi qui vous parle" (But me, I who am
speaking to you) (174/119). Moi, in a wedding dress, then addresses Ateba,
identifying herself as her soul. As Ateba advances toward the light, she
brings the legend to its desired conclusion—that is, the promised return to
a female utopia. One of the lessons offered by the novel is that women must
take responsibility for their own lives by freeing themselves.

"Double *auteur(ité)*" in *C'est le soleil qui m'a brûlée* occurs in the guise
of Moi, who speaks in the first person for Ateba, whose subaltern position
denies her voice. Moi, therefore, is the author of her story. Their "marriage" at the close of the narrative symbolizes their synthesis into one
single being.

Like Ateba, Claire Clamont in Marie Chauvet's *Amour* is without parents, single, exploited, a virgin, and a writing subject who kills a symbol of women's oppression. Claire, however, comes from an aristocratic Haitian family and at age thirty-nine, feels as if she is a spectator to her own life, a kind of disembodiment that is configured as the witness/narrator Moi in *C'est le soleil qui m'a brûlée*. The resemblance between the two texts does not stop there. Not only is Beyala's title actually inscribed in *Amour*, the poem taken from the Bible's Song of Songs also resonates in this text. In response to Félicia's question about her sister Claire's dark skin, their mother explains that it is the sun that made her that way: "Le soleil l'a un peu brûlée" (119). Displaced by her color, Claire's name is, consequently, ironic in that she is not light-skinned as her name indicates (peau claire = light skinned; peau foncée = dark skinned). Claire is marginalized within her own family and community, a society where race, class, color, and gender are crucial in determining one's place.[6]

Claire locates herself on the periphery: invisible, lucid, dangerous, unmarried, childless, an "old maid," she calls herself, mockingly, in that order, as the narrative opens. She relishes this status because no one detects her secret power as a spy and manipulator: "Je fais le guet. Je suis dans les coulisses et ils me croient inexistante. C'est moi le metteur en scène du drame. Je les pousse sur la scène, adroitement, sans avoir l'air d'intervenir et cependant, je les manoeuvre" (I spy. I am backstage and they believe that I do not exist. I am the director. I push them on the stage, adroitly, without seeming to intervene, but nevertheless, I maneuver them) (12). Claire is at once director and spectator: "J'avais évolué comme distincte de mon moi actuel: spectatrice étonnée de ma propre vie" (I had evolved distinctly from my present self; surprised spectator of my own life) (142). Moreover, like an actor, she wears a mask, albeit figurative, a choice she later questions: "Je surveille chacune de mes expressions, chacune de mes attitudes. Vais-je jusqu'à la fin de ma vie porter ce masque étouffant?" (I watch each one of my expressions, each attitude. Will I wear this stifling mask for the rest of my life?) (176). Chauvet's choice of a theater metaphor reproduces Frantz Fanon's trope of colonialism as a *drame absurde*, but in a neocolonial context.[7] Claire's impersonations render her invisible, allowing her to construct an identity that permits her to circulate with confidence: "Qui jamais se méfiera de moi? C'est là ma force" (who will ever distrust me? That is my strength) (159); "Je suis si terne que j'en deviens incolore" (I am so colorless that I become transparent) (148).

Claire's invisibility is complemented by her voicelessness. Upon meeting Jean Luze for the first time, she responds to his question by pointing.

On another occasion he astutely remarks that her unwillingness to answer questions directly is a tactic to discourage the curious. In the company of Jean and his friends, Claire listens quietly without participating in the conversation. She would also silently set the table and serve her suitor, Justin Rollier, as her sisters entertained him. When Claire does dare speak, however, she is often interrupted. Silence for Claire, however, can function as a weapon. Although she suspects that Annette is having an affair with Félicia's husband, she decides to keep her suspicions to herself, her silence concealing feelings of revenge.

Nevertheless, inwardly burning, outwardly wearing a mask, Claire boasts in her diary about her power. The attentive reader, however, discerns the hollowness of her claims. Claire busies herself with "woman's work" (sewing, for example) in order to appear inconspicuous, but her desire for invisibility is not always intentional. Despite the fact that her dark skin makes her stand out, those around her often do not notice her or simply ignore her. Her sisters—eight years separate Claire from Félicia, and Félicia from Annette—treat her more like a servant than the person in charge of the household. They talk about her in her presence as if she were not there. Madame Camuse even talks about Claire in the past tense.

Although *Amour* is set between 1900 and 1939, when various groups vied for power in Haiti, the stifling atmosphere of the predatory state—in the form of surveillance, corruption, and injustice—reproduces the oppressive conditions under the Duvalier regime of the 1960s. Chauvet herself was harassed to the point where her novel was ridiculed in the press, taken off the market, and she was forced to flee Haiti.[8]

It is intriguing to read Claire's desired invisibility and the Haitian government's exertion of authority through Foucault's analysis of power relations in the prison system. He writes that beginning in the nineteenth century, the spectacle of public correction was replaced by a hierarchical system of constraints, based on surveillance: "Disciplinary power . . . is exercised through its invisibility; at the same time it imposes on those whom it subjects a principle of compulsory invisibility. In discipline, it is the subjects who have to be seen. Their visibility assures the hold of the power that is exercised over them" (187).

Claire does manage to achieve invisibility, most often not through her own efforts, but this attempt to appropriate power is futile. On the other hand, those in power profit from the advantages of invisibility. Although Port-au-Prince, the country's capital, is located far away from the provincial town where the novel is set, the government's power is manifested locally through its low-level enforcers, informants, and Calédu, the town's police chief. They form a network representing the interests of the state, spy on the citizens, and mete out punishment behind prison walls. The threat of intervention or constraint on the populace is constant.

According to Foucault, subjects are visible. In *Amour*, characters engage in seeing without being seen, a major activity. Reclusive Claire barricades herself behind the double-locked door of her bedroom. From the window she witnesses Calédu beating citizens,[9] observes farmers whom she employs protest against her low coffee prices, and spies on Annette and her lover, Bob Charivi. She eavesdrops on Jean Luze and Félicia, rummaging through their drawers like the police had done to terrorize the bourgeoisie, confiscating their weapons. She watches Jean Luze and Annette through a keyhole, suspecting they are having an affair. Claire's surveillance was passed down, one can say, from her parents, who rigidly controlled her every move and choice of reading material. The Clamonts are not the only spies. Neighbors watch as Claire leaves her house to run to help Dora Soubiran, who has fallen in the street. Some beggars then stand on tiptoe to peer into Dora's house and then follow Claire home with their eyes. Neighbors monitor the comings and goings at Jane Bavière's house at night. Mothers routinely spy on their daughters. Certain beggars, with concealed weapons supplied by the police, spy on their fellow citizens. The objective of this constant surveillance is control. The allusion to mosquitoes who breed in the dirty water of the sidewalk cracks of the main street reproduces the situation in Haiti. The reader is invited to make the connection between the informants who resemble mosquitoes (and by extension, vampires) in that they suck human blood. It is significant, then, that the local enforcer, Calédu, whose identity is hidden behind a nickname, is killed by Claire with a stake-like dagger.

Claire's claustrophobic space, her *sanctuaire*, a microcosm of the town, is reproduced throughout the narrative, as most of the action takes place indoors. Women hide their faces in their handkerchiefs when Calédu shoots Jacques Marti in the street. Neighbors then peer from behind shutters and dusty curtains as Joël Marti recovers his brother's body. The entire community hides behind a facade: "nous nous abritons derrière une façade" (we seek shelter behind a facade) (34). Even a visit to the big city Port-au-Prince is experienced by the reader from inside Félicia's hospital room and Jean Luze's car.

Place and space matter in *Amour*. Everyone lives behind closed doubled-locked doors, be they bedrooms or jail cells. The resulting geography of terror on the citizenry that is enforced by the local authorities, the police, and their collaborators is aided by nature, with its alternating drought and hurricanes, destroying people and property. The forests are also victims of terrorism, raped for profit by Monsieur Long, who defrauds the peasants and then ships the trees overseas at enormous profit. Like the women, the trees are vulnerable to physical violation.

One site of resistance is Jane Bavière's house. It is there that the opposition meets in secret under the cover of darkness. It is significant that the Clamont residence is located between the houses of Jane Bavière and Dora Soubiran. These two rebels, Claire's contemporaries whom she abandoned long ago due to family pressure, provide models of female conduct. Jane defies local custom by becoming an single mother. Making a living as a seamstress, she can stand in her doorway with her son, refusing invisibility. Dora Soubiran also asserts her independence. A very religious woman, she is arrested and tortured by Calédu for refusing to accept his authority over God's. Claire, discouraged by her priest and Félicia from rekindling these friendships, makes the decision to leave the enclosed space of her room and venture outside to reclaim them: "Je ne les abandonnerai plus" (I will abandon them no longer) (172).[10] It is one step in her evolution.

Tropes of enclosure alternate with tropes of escape. Due to its architecture and location, the Clamont dining room is another site of resistance. Its door, opening to a patio, provides a border between inside and outside, connecting private and public space. It is through that door that Pierrilus enters without being seen to meet secretly with Jean Luze, Joël Marti, and the opposition group. It is also in the dining room where Jean Luze confides in Claire about his refusal to join Monsieur Long in his scam to defraud the poor. Jean and Claire develop a close relationship in the dining room, observing local businessmen outside bickering, blaming each other for their failure. One can read Claire's physical attraction to her brother-in-law Jean, a Frenchman, whose last name Luz etymologically translates as "light" (and thus complements her own name), as her unconscious desire for enlightenment, knowledge, and truth. Most important, Claire crosses the dining room, passes through its door to stab Calédu, who had sought refuge on the Clamont property.

Things are not what they seem. Artificial flowers adorn the religious procession. Monsieur Trudor earns a modest salary as the new *préfet* but lives in the only newly built mansion in town. Doctor Audier smiles at local officials in order to conceal his contempt for them. Behind Gisèle Audier's angelic demeanor lies a snob and gossip. Corrupt people appear angelic in church. Claire, with her repressed sexual desires, comments that priests hide their own behind their robes, and nuns' behind their veils.

Sometimes what is not hidden, people still refuse to see. Claire passes

Calédu on the street but pretends not to see him. Annette suggests playing music loud enough at Claire's birthday party to drown out screams emanating from the nearby prison. Everyone ignores the beggars: "Chacun feint de ne pas les voir" (everyone pretends not to see them) (13). This situation locates the town's complicity in its own subjugation. Other characters misread signs. Claire mistakenly waters an artificial plant. The town suspects that men visiting Jane Bavière's house at night are customers frequenting a prostitute. They are, in fact, activists plotting the overthrow of the regime.

What is concealed, however, can rise to the surface and explode. Claire's color, for example, the legacy of a long-forgotten brown-skinned ancestor, caused her shame as a youngster because it clashed with the rest of the family and their friends, who were white or very light skinned. Second, the darkness of night does not prevent Claire from hearing Dora crying next door after being whipped by Calédu. Neither are those detainees who remain in the prison seen by the public, but their screams can also be heard, haunting Claire and the text, as do the sounds of electric saws cutting down precious trees in a virtual slaughter.

Those who refuse voicelessness are punished for their audacity. A beggar who dares claim wages from Calédu suffers a beating at his hands. Intellectuals and poets are routinely singled out for harsh treatment, as their voices can be heard through writing. Agnès Grandupré, Tonton Mathurin, and Violette stand up despite the consequences. Young Agnès is ostracized for visiting outspoken Tonton Mathurin but still attends mass: "elle se tenait très droite, le menton fièrement relevé" (she stood very straight, her chin up, proudly) (129). Although masked men kidnap and beat Tonton Mathurin for criticizing candidate Henri Clamont, he remains defiant, nevertheless, positioning himself in the middle of the street to denounce the status quo. Violette, marginalized because she is a prostitute, boldly follows the public procession of Jacques Marti's casket to the cemetery.

I mentioned above Claire's hesitation when it comes to oral communication. Like Ramatoulaye, her achievement of voice comes in stages. At first, she cannot bring herself to tell Violette, the prostitute, that she admires her. Gradually, her muffled voice—"Ils m'empêchent d'ouvrir la bouche pour exprimer mes idées alors qu'elles m'étouffent" (they prevent me from opening my mouth in order to express my ideas when they stifle me) (152)—is transformed into a yell as she shouts at the street beggars to let Dora pass through. Still, Claire is not completely free to express herself. When Jane and her son mysteriously disappear in the middle of the night, most likely arrested by the police, she wants to scream, but cannot: "Je pense à Jane. Je pense à son petit et j'ai envie de hurler" (I think about Jane. I think about her young son and I feel like yelling) (183). In spite of Claire's coming late to speech, she has for a long time been articulate, but through writing. She used to keep a notebook, which was the only outlet available to her because of her class and gender, as Janis Mayes concludes (83). But she was punished by her father for doodling.

The female body in *Amour* is subject to various degrees of violation as we saw in *C'est le soleil qui m'a brûlée*. As a site of oppression, it is incapacitated, banished, beaten, exchanged, and put on display. Pregnancy, traditionally desired in women's culture, is rather an intrusion on Félicia's body, which nearly rejects one of its own biological functions. Jane Bavière's pregnancy is also accompanied by serious complications; she is exiled to the poor section of town by her family. Young Agnès Grandupré is beaten by her parents for transgressing society's boundaries when she visits radical Tonton Mathurin's home. Adult Dora Soubiran's genitals are targeted by Calédu for such a harsh beating that one month after her release, she still waddles when she walks.

Claire's body deserves special consideration and analysis because it undergoes different forms of abuse. Her father, disappointed that she was not a boy, takes his wrath out on her by beating her unmercifully. He reluctantly prepares Claire to inherit his estate and puts her on display on a visit to his coffee plantation on her thirteenth birthday to introduce her as his rightful heir. In the matter of marriage, Henri Clamont considers Claire's body a unit of exchange, not ruling out attracting a potential husband with a large dowry. He will resort to buying a mate for Claire as easily as he bought votes in the presidential elections. After her father's death, Claire's body is literally and figuratively held captive by Calédu. Trying to free herself from his gaze when their paths cross accidentally, and from his tight grasp while they dance at a ball, represents Claire's attempt to create her own space away from patriarchal authority.

Clothing functions as an important signifier in the text. Calédu's uniform permits him access to circles from which he would be excluded because of his class. Claire is embarrassed when her father insists that they don riding outfits imported from France, illustrating his adoption of European standards, what Jean Price-Mars labels *bovarysme collectif,* on their trip to his coffee plantation. That the plume on Claire's headpiece gets caught on a tree branch signals the absurdity of wearing such an outfit in the Haitian countryside. Adult Claire wears clothes that are designed to cover her body—long-sleeved outfits with a high collar—functioning as an extended mask, a costume, rendering her invisible, thus impermeable to the male gaze. She refuses to wear a bathing suit at the Trudors' pool party and is uncomfortable at the sight of the other exposed female bodies. Ill at ease with the public display of sexuality, she wanders into the library, only to notice an edition of Gustave Flaubert's *Salammbô*, which depicts the title character nude with a multicolored snake wrapped around her. The book is made of Moroccan leather, the heroine is Tunisian. The juxtaposition of the two female bodies, one naked, recalling another brown-skinned woman, Josephine Baker, who was similarly "on display" in Europe at the time of the novel, and one overdressed (Claire), renders more acute black women's objectification by the male gaze. Claire's almost complete and deliberate *re*-covering makes a strong statement about reclaiming the female body to conceal it from patronizing gazes as well as surveillance and control.

In the meantime, Claire projects her erotic fantasies onto Annette, appropriating her body, which is a younger version of her own: "J'ai besoin d'elle pour me servir d'intermédiaire" (I need her to serve as an intermediary) (50). Claire imagines herself in control of Annette's voice, of being her ventriloquist: "Elle parle pour moi. Lui ai-je mis ces mots dans la bouche?" (She speaks for me. Did I put these words in her mouth?) (24). Through this repossession, Claire lives vicariously through her flirtatious sister, who has a succession of lovers: "Elle avait osé ce que moi, son aînée de seize ans, je n'avais jamais pu" (she dared do what I, older by sixteen years, could never do) (140). Otherwise, Claire must settle for the pornographic postcards that she purchased clandestinely and hides under her bed along with the romance novels and her copy of *Lady Chatterly's Lover,* from which she memorizes passages: "c'est mon aphrodisiaque" (it is my aphrodisiac) (46).

At age thirty-nine Claire despairs being single and childless and imagines herself in a world of marriage and motherhood. When she was a child, the idea of marriage meant freedom from her parents' surveillance and tyranny. As she gets older, Claire becomes convinced that marriage and a family are essential to her happiness. They become her obsession and symbolize her acceptance of Haitian society's expectation of women of her social class. She is understandably disappointed when her suitor, Justin Rollier, is attracted to Annette instead. Their wedding does not take place, however, as Rollier dies from pneumonia. When Jean Luze and Félicia marry, Claire envies his devotion to her sister to the point of planning her death in order to take her place in his life. The text is clearly critical of Claire's obsession with marriage, showing that in a community such as hers, it is not necessarily in the best interests of women. One example is that Jane's fiancé dies in a car accident, leaving her pregnant and vulnerable to society's condemnation. Marriage's patriarchal ideology re-creates the structure of the state. Her own mother did not dare question her husband, Henri's, decisions, even though they came close to ruining the family financially.

As far as motherhood is concerned, Claire has had substantial experience. With each new child, her mother's dependency on her increased, especially three months after Henri's death, when Annette was born. Claire was nineteen, Félicia eleven, and Annette three when Claire assumed full control over the raising of her sisters when their mother died. Claire's "other mother" status did not diminish when her sisters reached adulthood. Claire attends to Félicia during her two pregnancies, the second one being so difficult that Claire was asked to accept full responsibility for her nephew Jean-Claude, even keeping the child in her own room. Nonetheless, all of those years of experience do not suffice:

> Je ne veux pas d'un enfant qui m'appartienne au quart, mais d'un qui soit tout à fait à moi. Je ne veux pas m'attacher à ceux des autres. Quoique la vie m'ait tout refusé, je n'ai aucune disposition pour jouer les mères adoptives. J'embrasse les bonnes joues rondes du fils de Jane mais je reste libre devant lui, les portes de mon coeur aussi solidement barricadées que celles de ma chambre.

> (I do not want a child who belongs to me one fourth, but one who belongs to me entirely. I do not want to attach myself to others' children. Although life has denied me everything, I do not have the disposition to play adoptive mother. I kiss Jane's sons' round cheeks, but I remain free, the doors to my heart as solidly barricaded as those to my bedroom.) (68)

Claire wants to have a child of her own, to reproduce herself. Afraid of the scandal that would ensue if she had a child without being married (for that reason Claire finds Jane Bavière so courageous), she spends hours in her room cradling a doll she calls Caroline, not surprisingly an approximate anagram of Claire.

One can conclude that marriage and motherhood are an ideal to which Claire aspires. When Félicia is bedridden in the early months of her second pregnancy, Claire becomes a pseudo-wife to Jean Luze as well as a surrogate mother to Jean-Claude, to the point of hoping that he will call her mother. Convinced that she is not playing a role—"je suis effectivement mère et épouse" (I am actually a mother and wife) (169–70)—but not daring to utter those words out loud, she fumes when Annette teases her.

Books and libraries, reading and writing are as central to *Amour* as they are in *Une si longue lettre* and *C'est le soleil qui m'a brûlée*. While the books in the Trudors' extensive library are on display simply to impress visitors, Jean Luze's collection serves a more useful purpose. Claire borrows from it regularly, relishing the freedom to choose her own reading material, and thus countering her parents' early control over her choice of texts. Censorship, however, is practiced by the government on a larger scale. Writers are routinely harassed and imprisoned, so Claire realizes the dangers of literacy: "Poussez de hauts cris si jamais ce manuscrit vous tombe sous les yeux" (scream as loud as you can if this manuscript falls into your hands) (34), but after discovering her talent for writing—"J'ai pris conscience de moi" (I became aware of myself) (10)—she becomes arrogant and decides to keep a journal, recording her observations and the activities of those around her.[11] *Amour,* in fact, is composed of fragments that resemble undated and unsigned entries in a diary, except for a flashback that takes up a good deal of the narrative, and ends with the arrival to the town of Calédu: "me voilà revenue au présent" (here I am back in the present) (142). Claire had been discouraged from writing, her voice silenced since her father punished her for what he termed "doodling." Writing in this case then takes the place of speech, for Claire used to avoid expressing herself orally—"moi qui évite de parler" (I who avoid speaking) (25). Claire's pen substitutes for her voice. Later, contentment, which she equates with simulated motherhood and wifehood, replaces the desire to write: "Voilà un mois que je n'ai rien ajouté à mon journal. Je n'en ai eu ni le temps ni l'envie. Ma vie est si bien remplie! J'ai un fils et un homme. Ma porte est ouverte tout le jour à Jean Luze. Pourquoi aurais-je besoin d'un exutoire? Je vis pleinement" (It has been a month since I have written anything in my diary. I have had neither the time nor the inclination. My life is so full! I have a son and a man. My door is open all day to Jean Luze. Why would I need an outlet? My life is full) (161). Claire's diary comes to an end when she kills Calédu. Again, inscribing her voice is no longer necessary, as it has been replaced by an act of resistance.

Amour, the title of Chauvet's novel, suggests heartfelt feelings and positive emotions. Love, however, in the perverse universe of *Amour* is tantamount to suffering and lack, causing one to become sadistic and cruel: "comme l'amour rend sadique et cruel!" (how love renders sadistic and cruel!) (103). The novel is full of sexual longings, mostly unfulfilled.[12] Because of her Catholic education, Claire is confused about erotic love, cynically defining it in terms of a physical activity devoid of emotion: "l'amour n'est que le frottement de deux parcelles de chair" (love is only the rubbing together of two parcels of flesh) (83). Claire's one chance at love is subverted by her internalization of European standards of beauty, which leads her to break off the relationship with Frantz Camuse, assuming that he will never marry her. Repulsed by the contrast between her hand and his lighter colored one, Claire in this scene resembles Ourika. Aware that skin color in Haiti is a signifier of superiority/inferiority, she has experienced how it has marked her life. It is the root cause of the jealousy and hatred she feels toward Félicia, whose white skin afforded her privileges she herself does not enjoy. Platonic love is not an adequate replacement.

At the close of *Amour,* Claire's body becomes unrecognizable to her. Looking in the mirror:

> Je me découvre, surprise, un faciès asymétrique: profil gauche, rêveur, tendre; profil droit, sensuel, féroce. Est-ce moi ou ce que je vois de moi? Mes mains aussi me semblent, tout à coup, dissemblables; celle faite pour agir, plus épaisse, plus lourde. Pourquoi ai-je dans la bouche le goût de fiel?

> (Surprised, I discover that I have asymmetrical features; left profile, dreamy, tender; right profile, sensual, ferocious. Is it me or what I see of myself? Suddenly, my hands also seem to be completely dissimilar. This one made to act, is thicker, heavier. Why do I have the taste of bile in my mouth?) (185)

This fragmented body will kill Calédu and is reminiscent of Ateba's response in *C'est le soleil qui m'a brûlée.* Claire thus evolves from a *vieille fille,* as she calls herself at the opening of *Amour,* to a "radical spinster," a progression Laura Doan defines as from "powerless other to self empowering subject" (15). That Claire, the sexually deviant unmarried female (borrowing Doan's description), murders Calédu, qualifies her for that status.

Amour clearly critiques institutions that limit opportunity and suppress freedom in Haiti. Claire successfully transgresses those boundaries. Her muffled voice finds expression through writing and thereby subverts censorship. Her repressed sexual desire seeks release through Annette. However, Claire's act of resistance—stabbing the government's representative, Calédu—remains ambiguous, as afterward she returns to her locked bedroom without joining the protesters outside. In *C'est le soleil qui m'a brûlée,* Ateba's lack of voice is reproduced in the structure of the novel; Moi speaks for her. Like Claire, she writes in secret; but realizing that writing is a skill that has no useful purpose, she tears up the letters she composes to women and to God. Her repressed sexual desire finds an outlet in prostitution, a degrading profession practiced by Betty, Ekassi, and Irène, which is a metaphor for some women's condition in contemporary Cameroonian inner cities. That Ateba kills her anonymous customer changes absolutely nothing. We are indeed a long way from "Nguessi Ngonda," whose message is that women's goals can be achieved through determination and cooperation.

With Calixthe Beyala's *C'est le soleil qui m'a brûlée* and Marie Chauvet's *Amour,* Haiti and Cameroon intersect symbolically as both authors, considered controversial in their home countries for their outspokenness, create protagonists silenced by society, seek refuge in an interior space, finally break free, and perform an act of violent resistance. Although the characters do not often speak out loud, their voices emanate from Ateba's and Claire's diary, respectively. In the next chapter, I discuss the inscriptions of women's voices in life stories where authorship should not be ambiguous.

6

Women's Life Stories as Historical Voice

Femme d'Afrique: La vie d'Aoua Kéita racontée par elle-même and Dany Bébel-Gisler's *Léonora: L'histoire enfouie de la Guadeloupe*

Ecrire ne tue pas la voix, mais la réveille, surtout pour ressusciter tant de soeurs disparues.

(Writing does not silence the voice, but awakens it, above all to resurrect so many vanished sisters.)

Assia Djebar, *L'amour, la fantasia*

Voilà que cette histoire des origines, cette histoire qui ne reposait que sur le dire, la parole des uns et des autres, rentrait dans la réalité. Elle n'attendait plus que la main d'un scribe pour la fixer par écrit et ainsi lui donner la pesanteur de la vérité.

(Now this story of origins, this story based only on saying, on the word of one and the other, was becoming reality. It now asks only for a scribe's hand to set it in writing and thus give it the gravity of truth.)

Maryse Condé, *Désirada*

Dans la langue de mon île, je crie ma volonté et le chant de ces mots trop longtemps étouffés fait affluer les souvenirs.

(In the language of my island, I shout my will and the singing of these too long muffled words makes memories flow.)

Michèle Maillet, *Bonsoir, faites de doux rêves!*

Much has changed since Jean-Pierre Makouta-Mboukou asserted in 1980 that autobiography in francophone Africa was a neglected genre (183), and since my research on women autobiographers began in 1990. There has been a steady increase in the number of life stories by African women and especially in the number of studies of the genre. In the summer 1997 issue of *Research in African Literatures* devoted to autobiography, seven of the nine essays are centered on women's self-stories and six of those feature francophone subjects.[1] There are fewer autobiographies from the francophone Caribbean; women writers seem to prefer the novel form.[2] Nevertheless, to say that Kesso Barry's *Kesso: Princesse peuhle*, Andrée

Blouin's *My Country, Africa,* Michèle Maillet's *Bonsoir, faites de doux rêves!,* and Odet Maria's *Une enfance antillaise* inscribe a woman's voice is redundant, as autobiographies obviously utilize the first person. I suggest that African and Caribbean women appropriate orality as a strategy for their life stories, inscribing their voices in a particular way. Speech patterns and call-and-response modes function to engage the reader in a dialogue with the author. Moreover, Aoua Kéita in *Femme d'Afrique: La vie d'Aoua Kéita racontée par elle-même* (1975) and Dany Bébel-Gisler in *Léonora: L'histoire enfouie de la Guadeloupe* (1985), in particular, postulate a correspondence between their individual stories and national history. Indeed, *histoire* in French is defined as story as well as history, in this case "herstory," and Kéita chronicles the founding of the Republic of Mali. As a member of the Union Soudanaise of the Rassemblement Démocratique Africain (USRDA), she not only played an important role in the struggle for independence, but she inscribes women's participation as well.

Correspondence, with its resonance of writing, is another operative word. By translating and transcribing Léonora's story from Creole into French, Dany Bébel-Gisler creates a space for a Creole-speaking rural woman who quit school at age fourteen to speak to an audience to whom she would not ordinarily have access. In subtitling Léonora's text "The Buried (His)story of Guadeloupe," Bébel-Gisler equates Léonora's life, not extraordinary or public, like that of Aoua Kéita, with the island's history, which the author excavates. That life stories depend on the subject's memory connects to Trinh T. Minh-ha's assertion that women's memories are "the world's earliest archives or libraries," a statement which expands Amadou Hampaté Bâ's claim about male traditionalists (121). The implication is that women through their voices are one repository of history whether notable or not. Life stories providing a gendered historical voice characterizes both *Léonora* and *Femme d'Afrique.*

Aoua Kéita associates voice, writing, and nation building, encouraging workers, especially activists, to put their own stories on paper in order to document history for the young:

> les travailleurs, même dans la vieillesse, peuvent continuer à apporter une contribution effective à la construction du pays. En effet, ces hommes, surtout ceux ayant un certain niveau intellectuel, débarrassés de toutes préoccupations matérielles, peuvent réfléchir, concevoir et écrire leurs expériences multiples et riches en événements. Ces documents mis en forme par nos enfants plus lettrés, peuvent constituer un trésor historique pour les générations futures.

(workers, even in old age, can continue to contribute effectively to the development of the country. These men, especially those who have attained a certain intellectual level and rid of all material preoccupations, can reflect, conceive and write their numerous rich experiences. These documents set down by our more literate children can constitute an historical treasure for future generations.) (239)

Aoua Kéita does not have to resort to her prescription for assuring the recording of significant experiences—that is, having someone else transcribe her story. *Femme d'Afrique: La vie d'Aoua Kéita racontée par elle-même* (1975) inscribes her own voice and at once proclaims its difference from the numerous books on the market about Africa and Africans, which will be discussed below. Kéita's title "Woman of Africa" affirms her gender and identifies her with the entire continent. Inscribing herself in the subtitle, "The life of Aoua Kéita *told by herself*" (emphasis added), and on the title page, where she also lists her affiliations, calls attention to the speaking/writing subject, which is reinforced by the cover of the second edition, a photograph of her sitting in her office surrounded by books piled high on a table and reading. The four-hundred-page narrative, covering the years 1931 to 1960, in chronicling her life as a midwife, deputy, and member of the national political office of the Union Soudanaise du Rassemblement Démocratique Africain, the political party fighting for liberation, also charts the anticolonial struggle for an independent Mali.

The visual representation of written discourse on the cover is balanced by Kéita's privileging in the first few pages of women transmitting knowledge orally. The first chapter, titled "Une éducation soudanaise traditionnelle" (a traditional Sudanese education), includes two tales told by her mother, whom she recalls relating tales at night around the fire to teach life's lessons to the children of her father's other wives, friends, *griots*, and servants. At times, women related specific stories to girls that were designed to make them obedient and respectful. One tale Kéita's mother related centers on Diadiaratou, a disobedient daughter who rebuffs the suitors approved by her family, choosing to marry out of love a handsome stranger named Zoumana, who later abandons her in the forest. Rescued by her brother, Diadiaratou learns her lesson in the end.

Aoua Kéita describes her mother as being profoundly traditionalist, not wanting her daughter to attend the French school: "Pour elle, la place d'une jeune fille, d'une future femme, était au foyer et non à l'école dont la fréquentation pouvait porter ombrage à la moralité" (for her, a girl's place, a future woman's place was in the home and not in school where attendance could offend moral standards) (28). In a society where the mother exercised authority over the education of her children, Aoua's mother's power in this area was usurped by her husband, who, in 1923, when Aoua was ten, enrolled her in the Orphelinat des Métisses, the French school for girls. Fortunately, the early moral and *oral* education Kéita received at home also sustained her throughout the three years she spent at the Ecole de Médecine de Dakar, where she trained to be a midwife. However, Diadiaratou's fictional experience resonates in Kéita's real life when she marries a man of her own choice, despite her mother's wish that she marry a relative, a tailor. After fourteen years her marriage ends in divorce.

Kéita speaks only briefly—three sentences—about the years she spent at medical school in Dakar between 1928 and 1931, signifying her desire to focus on political rather than personal issues. The rest of the narrative—beginning with chapter 2—is centered on her work as a midwife and *militante* (activist) with the USRDA, which was launched by her marriage to Dr. Daouda Diawara in 1935. They both became involved in voter registration and campaign work to get USRDA candidates elected to the French National Assembly. As a result, members of the group experienced harassment, sabotage, firings, and even exile. Kéita's profession afforded her constant contact with women whose confidence and trust she gained readily. She was thus able to form women's groups that sometimes evolved into an arm of the USRDA. Because of her political activity, Kéita was frequently transferred by the colonial government to posts in and around Senegal, Guinea, French Sudan, and France. Each transfer, however, brought her new opportunities to organize and recruit women to the cause. Her chosen task was to improve women's roles in society: "Et j'ai soutenu et continue à soutenir la thèse selon laquelle l'évolution d'un pays est fonction de la place que les femmes occupent dans la vie publique de ce pays" (I supported and continue to support the thesis that the evolution of a country is a function of the place that women occupy in the public life of that country) (240). This comment discloses Kéita's desire to expand women's authority to the public sphere.

What makes *Femme d'Afrique* unique for its time is its recording of the particular experiences of a politically active woman. Not only did she experience discrimination and segregation like her male counterparts in a colonial society, she faced other obstacles as well because of her gender. In the early years, her husband—even though he considered her an equal—recommended that she not speak up at meetings held in their house so as not to offend the men: "Diawara, très prudent et connaissant la mentalité des hommes, m'avait recommendé le silence pour ménager les susceptibilités des camarades qui certainement n'avaient jamais engagé de discussion avec une femme" (Diawara, very careful and knowing the male way of thinking, had recommended that I remain silent in order to spare the feelings of these male friends who had never been involved in a discussion with a woman) (55). During one election campaign in 1959, she was insulted by the Singné village chief and then run out of town. Another incident involved a man in Bissaou who was so surprised to meet a woman activist that it sparked this exchange: "'Chère Madame, je vous donne un conseil d'aîné: retirez-vous de la politique, elle n'est pas bonne pour les hommes et elle peut être fatale pour une femme'. 'Au revoir, Monsieur,' lui dis-je. 'Je ferai de la politique jusqu'au bout!'" ("Dear Madam, take this advice from an elder: get out of politics; it's not good for men and it could be fatal for a woman." "Goodbye, sir," I answered. "I will be involved in politics to the bitter end") (175–76). Because Kéita was a practicing Muslim, but single and childless, she encountered additional difficulties.

The women who joined her groups were also vulnerable to criticism. One was told by her husband to stay close to home: "'Tu ferais mieux d'aller faire ta cuisine au lieu de t'occuper de l'action d'autrui, la politique c'est l'affaire des hommes et non la tienne'" (You would be better off cooking instead of being involved in others' affairs; politics are for men and not for you) (56). Despite these obstacles, however, Kéita held secret meetings in the maternity hospital in Niono, where she explained voting procedures to women; formed a women's section of the local USRDA in Gao; was successful in organizing women's unions, the Mutuelle des Femmes de Nara in 1955 and the Intersyndicat des Femmes Travailleuses. As a committed unionist, she was a delegate representing the Union Générale des Travailleurs de l'Afrique Noire (African Workers Union) to the Fédération Syndicale Mondiale (World Federation of Unions) convention held in Germany in 1957. Finally, she was elected to the political bureau of the USRDA in 1958 on the eve of independence.

The text closes as independence is declared on September 22, 1960, but the narrator alludes to the continuing struggle for freedom, democracy, and universal peace. As a midwife/activist Aoua Kéita made her mark on the private and public spheres. Because *Femme d'Afrique* places so much emphasis on the activities of the USRDA, it can also be read as a chronicle of the birth of the Republic of Mali. It is a text functioning as both history and autobiography.

Aoua Kéita inscribed her own voice in her autobiography, but the model she suggested for recording her elders' experiences is unmistakably evident in *Léonora: L'histoire enfouie de la Guadeloupe,* a narrative transcribed and translated by Dany Bébel-Gisler, who makes a peasant Creole-speaking woman's voice accessible to the French-reading public. Some of the same issues of authorship that arise in some of the early African pseudo-autobiographies come into play here. Can *Léonora* really be considered an autobiography? Although *Léonora* is part of Segher's "mémoire vive" series, the front cover does not carry her signature. It is a first-person text, but it is not until the afterword that Bébel-Gisler explains that she listened to, transcribed, and translated the narrative by a Guadeloupean woman from the Lamentin region, the daughter of a sharecropper. *Autoethnography*, a term Françoise Lionnet uses in *Autobiographical Voices* to define a text in which a person relates a collective story rather than a private one, does not adequately capture the nuances in *Léonora*. One can justify *Léonora*, however, as a life story in which Dany Bébel-Gisler embodies Aoua Kéita's literate generation writing down the rich experiences of their elders.

Unlike books by anthropologists in which Europeans interviewed Africans, there is no difference in race, gender, or nationality between the scribe and the narrator in *Léonora*. In fact, Bébel-Gisler's role corresponds to that of the *marqueur de paroles* found in Edouard Glissant and Patrick Chamoiseau's novels. One important difference between *Léonora* and those texts, however, is that Bébel-Gisler remains outside of the narration; she is not a character in fiction. Nevertheless, the editors involved with the American translation of *Léonora* distance it from history and make three significant choices visible on the cover of the paperback edition. First, they title the text "The Buried *Story* of Guadeloupe" instead of "Buried History." Second, they attach the word *novel* to the title. Third, the cover pictures a Caribbean woman wearing a traditional madras and earrings. While the first two modifications accentuate the fictional aspects of the text, the picture of the older woman in national dress situates this narrator in a more authenticating *conte* than the French edition, which pictures on the front cover a sketch of a younger black woman whose straight hair and bangs do not immediately identify her as a Creole woman of a certain age.

I prefer to read *Léonora* as a life story that inscribes at least three women's voices. Léonora's long narrative is framed, on the one hand, by a tale about slaves' imaginary return to Africa in order to escape torture, as related by a ninety-eight-year-old Guadeloupean peasant woman. With its protocol of a storytelling session conserved—"Sété léstravay. C'était l'esclavage" (It was the time of slavery) (71)—the tale serves to situate Léonora's life in a historical context and immerses the reader in the distant past. The ellipses, question marks, and exclamation points simulate the woman's speaking voice, as does the Creole text in the left-hand column. The French translation in the right-hand column is provided for those who cannot read Creole. Dany Bébel-Gisler's voice emerges only at the end of the entire text, after Léonora has completed relating her story. In the afterword, Bébel-Gisler discloses how much Léonora's background and experiences resonate in her own life and her hope that this story of affirmation and resistance to French cultural imperialism will not only help Guadeloupeans know themselves better, but change the perception of Guadeloupe in the global imaginary. The notes provide a detailed explanation of Creole words and expressions.

In between the tale about triumph over suffering told by the older woman (Anmann) and the afterword by the scribe (Bébel-Gisler), resides Léonora's narrative, which dominates the text. Léonora is unquestionably the author of her own narrative:

> Il est déjà bien haut le cocotier que mes parents ont planté là où le cordon de mon nombril est enterré, dans le petit hameau qu'on appelle Carangaise, dans la commune de Capesterre-Belle-Eau, en Guadeloupe. C'est là que j'ai été élevée avec mes frères et soeurs, cinq garçons et quatre filles.

> (The coconut palm my parents planted is now quite tall, the one they planted on the spot where my umbilical cord is buried, in the hamlet of Carangaise, in the parish of Capesterre-Belle-Eau, in Guadeloupe. That's where I spent my childhood with my brothers and sisters, five boys and four girls.) (11/4)

In the succeeding fifteen chapters, Léonora, the daughter of a cane cutter, recounts the story of her survival under difficult circumstances: early family life in a small town with a strict and alcoholic father and hard-working mother; experiences at school; moving to the big city Pointe-à-Pitre, where she worked as a bookkeeper and rinser of soda bottles; mentoring by Cousine Amélya; returning to the countryside; voting for the first time; relationships with Alexander, father of her first two children; and husband Joseph, whom she married after they had six children; living and working on a plantation; the pressures of being the wife of a watchman who supports the cane workers' strike; the important place that religion began to occupy in her life; food shortages during World War II; and local elections—all from a woman's perspective.

As I mentioned above, this text is deeply rooted in orality. There are transcribed songs, learned at school and church, and tales, one of which is a lengthy and uninterrupted story recounted by Monsieur Fistibal involving a young female character named Persillette (22–33/13–22). Like Liking and Hourantier, Léonora, through Bébel-Gisler, incorporates the storytelling protocols. The call—"Yé krik!"—and response—"Yé krak!"—signaling the interaction between the *conteur* and audience, are retained. Man Bety is singled out as "une de nos 'grangrèk savann'—comme on appelle ici ces gens pleins de sagesse et de science. Leur instruction, ils ne l'ont pas prise à l'école, mais dans la vie et auprès des Anciens" (one of our *grangrèk savann*—as we call our wise men and women. Their learning doesn't come from school, but from life and the teachings of the elders) (66/48). Man Bety is such a good storyteller that Léonora loses track of time listening to her.

Léonora herself is an active participant in the oral tradition, her voice is heard around the community. Adept at riddles and word games, she distinguishes herself at wakes, a tradition in Carangaise that is rare in Grosse-Montagne (55–56/40). Léonora decides to participate in these *séances* (sessions), depending on the atmosphere of these mostly male gatherings. Other signs of orality in the text are her short sentences, frequent use of proverbs and aphorisms, and of the familiar *tu* (you) as a pronoun.

At the same time, Bébel-Gisler inserts Léonora's text into the written tradition, valorizing her voice and knowledge by affiliating them with established authorities in the public sphere. While the titles of the chapters are taken from Léonora's spoken words in Creole and then translated into French, most of the epigraphs are taken from nonfiction works that Léonora probably did not know: Frantz Fanon on freedom, James Baldwin on ancestral land, Jacques Lacan on madness, Père Dutertre on slavery, and Gérard Lauriette on schooling in Guadeloupe, an eighteenth-century Guadeloupean prosecutor on slave revolts, for example. Bébel-Gisler also chooses epigraphs from Caribbean novels, Jacques Roumain's *Gouverneurs de la rosée* and Simone Schwarz-Bart's *Pluie et vent sur Télumée Miracle*. It is significant that the last, culminating chapter, the one in which Bébel-Gisler records Léonora's finest triumph in 1975—"année de mes plus grandes joies comme de ma plus grande souffrance" (the year of my greatest joys as well as my greatest sorrows) (284/223)—is opened by an aphorism in Creole provided by Man Fofo, a Guadeloupean peasant woman. All of these "voices of *auteurité*/authority" introduce and confirm what Léonora will discuss in the chapter. Residing outside of and yet complementing her narrative, these epigraphs create a sort of oral/written interface without any hierarchy implied. Léonora's Guadeloupean and oral voice articulates the previously suppressed history inscribed in the subtitle

L'histoire enfouie de la Guadeloupe (The buried history of Guadeloupe). She and Dany Bébel-Gisler, who literally inscribes Léonora's voice, embody "double *auteur(ité)*."

These autobiographical narratives are personal stories by women not promoting themselves, as so many Western autobiographies, but rather providing another perspective on the African and Caribbean past. They document the experiences of women growing up in changing societies, lives that are average or privileged, sheltered or unprotected, rural or urban. Aoua Kéita challenges the destiny prescribed by a patriarchal tradition in orature. Becoming a wife who does not enter the public arena was too restrictive for her. Ironically, it was Kéita's father who insisted that she attend French school, which provided access to a broader world of travel and politics.

Francophone African and Caribbean women's life stories intersect with African American as well as other women's autobiographies in that they reveal concerns with documenting history, the collective experience, and family and gender issues. These life stories, which span the years of colonization, independence, and departmentalization, not only provide a fascinating counterpoint to the representations of women in orature, fiction, and popular culture, but they also allow women to speak for themselves. These women are wives, mothers, sisters, and daughters, but they are also independent and acquiescent, courageous and average, politically active and politically disinterested. They choose husbands without necessarily seeking their parents' permission. Some confront patriarchy and colonialism and others do not challenge it. They do not idealize motherhood, but recall its rewards as well as its tribulations. They do not fetishize the body. In short, they do not claim to present a monolithic "women's experience," but rather a variety of experiences.

African autobiography, in general, aims to document history for future generations as articulated by Nafissatou Diallo in the preface to *De Tilène au Plateau* (1975): "Le Sénégal a changé en une génération. Peut-être valait-il la peine de rappeler aux nouvelles pousses ce que nous fûmes" (Senegal has changed a lot in one generation. Perhaps it is worthwhile to remind the youth what we were). This concern with transmitting knowledge mirrors the traditional oral storyteller's objective.

As I mentioned above, francophone African and Caribbean life stories foreground women's voices. I would like to discuss briefly the ways in which some other autobiographies from these regions are informed by orality. Andrée Blouin's *My Country, Africa: Autobiography of the Black Pasionaria* (1983) carries on its title page "In collaboration with Jean

MacKellar," which indicates that it could have been transmitted orally in French and then translated into English. My inquiries to the publisher concerning the nature of the collaboration have not been answered. The presence of this other voice is problematic and raises questions of authorship,[3] unlike in *Léonora,* where Bébel-Gisler explains her contribution. Blouin herself inserts *My Country, Africa* into the oral tradition by imagining herself as the celebrant who customarily shares his/her life story with the attending guests: "If it were my turn to speak, I would tell of my sad years in the orphanage for girls of mixed blood . . . If it were my turn, I would speak of my precious children . . . I would speak of finding my true love . . . I would speak of an Africa. . ." (285). In four paragraphs she summarizes what she revealed in the entire text. This emphasis on speech and testimony reveals a side of history that had been buried: her difficult years between 1921 and 1962, as a *métisse* growing up in an orphanage run by the Order of Saint Joseph of Cluny in French Equatorial Africa. Her fourteen years there reveals that Christianity as practiced by the French was not a benevolent and enlightened gift to Africa, but clearly an arm of colonialism, both conspiring to oppress and exploit the local population. Blouin also provides facts about her participation in the independence movements in Guinea and the Congo, inscribing one woman's active involvement in this important process. Nafissatou Diallo is another autobiographer whose voice emerges. She enters into a dialogue with the reader, a collective body as evidenced by her use of the second person plural pronoun, *vous,* in her life story, *De Tilène au Plateau: Une enfance dakaroise* (1975), when she warns that the area where she was born no longer exists. Later on, she will again address her *Amis lecteurs* (friends/readers), who can empathize with her as she tries to express her feelings of loss—in a language that is not her own—when her father dies. Ken Bugul's autobiography, *Le baobab fou* (1982) opens with a legend about origins. The baobab tree in Senegal is the place where *griots* are buried, and thus symbolic of former lives and oral storytelling. *Kesso: Princesse peuhle* (1988) simulates a storytelling session in that the text is addressed to Kesso Barry's ten-year-old daughter, Sandra, whom she wants to *écouter* (listen) and *entendre* (hear) the story of her life that was "un combat que la femme en toi comprendra (a struggle that the woman in you will understand) (9). As a child, Kesso, despite her aristocratic origins, admired Madame Diala, a *griotte,* because her voice was a powerful instrument that could undo marriages and ruin reputations. She was in control, not only of her life, but could affect others' as well. For that reason Diala was feared. Orality informs the title of Michèle Maillet's *Bonsoir, faites de doux rêves! An-*

tillaise, speakerine . . . et remerciée! (1982), an autobiography written to explain to her fans the loss of her job as a television host. "Goodnight and sweet dreams" is how she closed each evening broadcast as a *speakerine*. While braiding her hair, Maillet's grandmother used to relate tales about a hairless dog, zombies, and *diablesses,* as well as stories about slavery, the slave trade, and colonialism, topics her father refused to discuss. With that background it is easy to understand, then, why it is her grandmother who is central to her reintegration into Martinican society after an absence of many years. Maillet's mother also participated in oral culture, telling Michèle stories and proverbs in Creole, a language her father rarely used.[4] Odet Maria re-creates a "séance de contes" (storytelling session) in *Une enfance antillaise: Voyage au fond de ma mémoire* (1992), by calling on her young readers to form a circle at her feet and listen to the story of her life, simulating what she would do in the evenings with her children and grandchildren, who now encourage her to tell those same stories to other children.

In contrast to life stories in which the author speaks for herself, early life histories of African women were collected orally and transcribed by European anthropologists, which problematizes authorship and voice. Jeanne-Françoise Vincent is listed as the author of *Traditions et transition: Entretiens avec des femmes Beti du Sud-Cameroun* (1976) (Traditions and transition: Interviews with Beti women from southern Cameroon), while I. Dugast, who during four consecutive evenings transcribed the life story of Kubong, a woman from the Ndogbiakat ethnic group, is listed as the author of "Autobiographie d'une femme banen." Anne Laurentin recorded the life stories of five women representing different social classes and generations in "Nzakara Women (Central African Republic)" and labels her work as biography, as does Helen Codere, *The Biography of an African Society, Rwanda, 1900–1960* (1973), which is composed of life histories of forty-eight people, among whom eleven are Tutsi women and eight are Hutu women. Benoît Verhaegen's *Femmes zaïroises de Kisangani: Combats pour la survie* (1990) contains twenty-nine accounts by urban women. Another interesting example is *Baba of Karo: A Woman of the Moslem Hausa* (1954). Mary Smith is listed as the author, but in the introduction her husband explains that while they were undertaking field research in Northern Nigeria, she conducted and recorded an interview with Baba over a six-week period between November 1949 and January 1950. He goes on to explain that the process involved sometimes asking questions to clarify meaning and later editorializing by filling in dates. In all of these examples the compiler's or scribe's voice is privileged over the speaking subject's voice. *Baba of Karo* as text adds still another layer of patriarchal discourse (in addition to colonial), in that a man is called on to validate two women's texts. This interference is characteristic of "as told to" autobiographies. Racial and cultural differences between the interviewer and the interviewee could also play a role in interpreting material. The line between biography and autobiography becomes blurred in these cases.[5]

The gender and racial gap are overcome by Awa Thiam, who frames her discussion around women's coming to voice in *La parole aux négresses* (1978) (Speak Out, Black Sisters). She interviewed approximately fifteen women from Senegal, Guinea, Mali, Nigeria, and the Congo: "Longtemps, les Négresses se sont tues: N'est-il pas temps qu'elles (re)découvrent leur voix, qu'elles prennent ou reprennent la parole?" (Black women have been silent for too long. Is it not high time that they discovered their own voices?) (17/11). The stories they tell, however, are anecdotal in nature, concern primarily relationships with men, and, therefore, are incomplete and cannot be considered life stories. What is especially relevant is that in one collective interview involving seven men and seven women, only two of the women expressed an opinion. Thiam astutely notes that their silence is rooted in intimidation.[6] France Alibar and Pierrette Lembeye-Boy's two-volume *Le couteau seul . . . sé kouto sèl . . .: La condition féminine aux Antilles* (1982) seeks to give women voice by weaving interviews with sixty-three Guadeloupean women of different social classes between the ages of fifteen and seventy-seven who talk about identity, schooling, sex education, single motherhood, and relationships with men. Carole Boyce Davies in "Collaboration and the Ordering Imperative in Life Story Production" astutely labels "crossover genre" such collective oral life stories.

These life stories inscribe, for the most part, unmediated voices, thus we have come a long way from the time when others spoke for women. They explain by example some African and Caribbean women's roles in society and document their perspectives on and participation in historical events, thereby giving the lie to imposed representations. Autobiographical voices inscribe subjectivity. These lives are and were witnesses to history, a history previously unrecorded but no less important. The authors function like "oralituraines," transmitting knowledge to future generations. Writing one's self—in this case, a real life—into history is empowering.

Conclusion

Malgré le doute, l'angoisse, j'écris maintenant les histoires que j'entends dans ma tête, sans retenue. Je n'ai aucune crainte. Je peux tout raconter.

(Despite doubt, anguish, I now write the stories I hear in my head, without restraint. I have no fear. I can relate everything.)

Jan J. Dominique, *Mémoire d'une amnésique*

African and Caribbean women's voices are inscribed on various sites: their bodies, pot lids, CDs, madras, *pagne,* and page. What these voices say subverts erasure, silence, and pervasive distorted constructions. Women fiction and nonfiction prose writers from Cameroon, Guadeloupe, Haiti, Mali, Martinique, and Senegal, all countries with strong literary traditions, allow women's perspectives to emerge by positioning their characters as tellers of their own stories, thereby providing women's perspectives on not only their own experiences, but also on a variety of issues in woman-centered/woman-narrated texts through double-voiced authority or "double *auteur(ité).*" These writers consciously appropriate the legacy of African and Caribbean "oralituraines," embracing their mission to transmit knowledge from generation to generation. These heirs publish tales told exclusively during girls' initiation ceremonies (Liking and Hourantier); incorporate into their texts characters who are *grandes conteuses,* like Reine Sans Nom, whose language is rich in proverbs and who every Thursday would relate tales (Schwarz-Bart); or *griottes* like Farmata, who possesses valuable knowledge about members of the community that no one else perceives (Bâ). The passing on of these skills is figured in the multigenerational characters of Toussine, Télumée, and Sonore in *Pluie et vent sur Télumée Miracle* or, for another example, from Creole-speaking Léonora to French-writing Dany Bébel-Gisler.

Women's voices, even as secondary characters, are clearly privileged in these texts. In *Une si longue lettre,* Ramatoulaye's unnamed grandmother's *sagesse* (wisdom) in the form of proverbs about raising children and motherhood sustains her in times of crisis. Although class conscious aristocrat Tante Nabou is Aïssatou's nemesis, she gives La Petite Nabou a traditional oral education before sending her to the French school in preparation for a useful career as a midwife. In *Femme d'Afrique* Sokona Diaouné confides to Aoua Kéita what Sarakolé mothers tell their daughters as they are initiated into the secret knowledge of *magnamagan*. All of these women participate in oral culture as "oralituraines" and serve as models for their "écrivaines" descendants.

Sidonie, Ramatoulaye, and Claire are fictional *écrivaines* whose voices emerge through their diaries. Whether their confinement is voluntary (Claire), involuntary (Sidonie), or a sign of respect for religion (Ramatoulaye), writing affords a space for introspection as well as a site from which to reach others. Sidonie writes for her son, from whom she has been separated, and for posterity, while Ramatoulaye inscribes her liberating coming-to-voice to her best friend, Aïssatou. Claire's complex narrative/diary in *Amour* serves as her confidant as well as a response to her father's characterization of her attempts at writing as doodling. While Ateba abandons writing to imaginary women, it is Moi through whom she achieves voice in *C'est le soleil qui m'a brûlée.*

"Nguessi Ngonda" and *Léonora* share the distinction of naming the central character in the title, but neither text carries that particular signature. The anonymous authors, the "oralituraines" of "Nguessi Ngonda," must rely on other women like Liking and Hourantier to keep the story alive, a story once restricted to a female audience during girls' initiation ceremonies. These rituals are no longer performed, but the inscription of these women's voices opens a window to Bassa women's culture. In a similar intergenerational transmission of knowledge, Dany Bébel-Gisler brings Léonora's story in her own words to the public. To transform oral texts in Bassa and Creole into written texts in French requires the work of a translator and a *marqueuse de parole,* such as Hourantier and Liking and Bébel-Gisler, who, unlike their male counterparts Edouard Glissant and Patrick Chamoiseau, do not inscribe themselves into the narrative.

Connecting women's written narratives across the diaspora with their gender-specific oral tradition which privileges their voices transmitting knowledge across generations was one of my objectives in this study. Francophone African and Caribbean women authors are anchored in orality. Their inscription of women's voices in both fiction and nonfiction marks a site of the convergence of telling and writing, as articulated by Mariama Bâ, as women define for themselves a space of indisputable authority. Gisèle Pineau summarizes this relationship between voice and inscription in the following manner: "Ecrire en tant que femme noire créole, c'est apporter ma voix aux autres des femmes d'ici et d'ailleurs qui témoignent pour demain, c'est donner à entendre une parole différente dans la langue française" (Writing as a black Creole woman is to bring my voice to other women's voices from here and elsewhere who bear witness for tomorrow; it is causing a different word to be heard in the French language) ("Ecrire" 295).

It is appropriate that at this point I revisit a few other points I made in the introduction. One, "Nguessi Ngonda" as character and text figures as a symbol of women's oral cultural heritage as well as an emblem of its legacy. Maryse Condé's short story "Trois femmes à Manhattan" (Three Women in Manhattan) embodies those issues in that it privileges women's voices, articulates the interplay between telling and writing—that is, oral and written discourses—emphasizes the transmission of knowledge between generations of women and positions female characters communicating across the diaspora. The three women alluded to in the title "Trois femmes à Manhattan" are all of African descent. Their lives intersect in one single location, rendering Manhattan a diasporic connection. They represent different generations of writers at different stages of their careers: Claude, the protagonist, is a nineteen-year-old Guadeloupean domestic worker and budding writer; her employer, Elinor, a hot young African American novelist; and Vera, an elderly Haitian journalist who reads her unpublished manuscripts aloud to her friend Claude. Vera is also Claude's inspiration, encouraging her to write. Although language is a problem—Elinor tries to communicate with Claude in French and Claude, in turn, cannot read Elinor's novels written in English—their adopted home, Manhattan, becomes the site of a legacy. These transnational fictional women writers, positioned as representing the past, the present, and the future, negotiate and navigate the spaces between oral and written texts like their counterparts in real life, who, by meticulously inscribing female voices, move toward subjectivity by assuming authority.

I began *Francophone Women Writers of Africa and the Caribbean* by quoting Mariama Bâ's lament about the lack of texts written by women despite the large number of stories they have to tell. It is fitting, then, that I conclude this study with a reference to the cover of her first novel, *Une si longue lettre*, which shows a black woman with pen in hand in the midst of writing. Not coincidentally, it is Ramatoulaye inscribing her voice in a letter to her best friend, Aïssatou. Furthermore, while Mariama Bâ's signature appears on her novel, her name is also inscribed on a plaque outside a school on Gorée Island named for her.[1] Gorée is itself a significant site of departure and of reunion for Africans and their descendants around the world.

Woman-centered/woman-narrated texts by women writers produce "double *auteurité*" and subvert the script imposed by orature, male writers, Western media, and popular culture. Female characters found in these texts are not all passive, silent, or helpless victims; nor are they idealized mothers, jealous wives, or disobedient daughters, as they are often represented. In fact, they represent a variety of women, most of whom are speaking subjects whose voices women authors inscribe.

Notes

Introduction

1. See the essays in *La civilisation de la femme dans la tradition africaine* and the article by Francesca Velayoudom Faithful.

2. Amadou Hampaté Bâ includes smiths and weavers in his category of traditionalists, but omits female crafts and professions.

3. The cover engraving of the profile of a black woman with a long ponytail and earrings on *Femmes: Livre d'or de la femme créole* is reproduced in part on the spine of each volume. Putting the six volumes together (re)forms the whole woman. Also, the letters spelling out FEMMES are printed on each spine.

4. Aminata Sow Fall created Editions du Centre Africain d'Echanges Culturels (CAEC), which has published several works by women, although it is not limited to women's works.

5. Marie Chauvet won the Prix de l'Alliance Française for *Fille d'Haïti* (1954) and the Prix France Antilles for *Fonds des Nègres* (1960). Marie-Thérèse Colimon won Le Prix France Haïti for *Fils de misère* (1974). *Femme d'Afrique: La vie d'Aoua Kéita racontée par elle-même* (1975) and Aminata Sow Fall's *La grève des bàttu* (The Beggars' Strike) (1979) were awarded the Grand Prix Littéraire de l'Afrique Noire. Aminata Sow Fall won the Prix International Alioune Diop for *L'appel des arènes* (1982) and Mariama Bâ earned the Prix Noma for *Une si longue lettre* (So Long a Letter) (1979). Simone Schwarz-Bart and Gisèle Pineau were awarded *Elle* magazine's literary prize for *Pluie et vent sur Télumée Miracle* (The Bridge of Beyond) and *La grande drive des esprits* (1993), respectively. Maryse Condé won the Anaïs Nin prize from the Académie Française for *La vie scélérate* (Tree of Life) (1987) and the grand prize for women for *Moi, Tituba, sorcière* (I, Tituba, Black Witch of Salem) (1986). In 1996, Calixthe Beyala was honored by the Académie Française for *Les honneurs perdus*.

6. See the proceedings edited by Phanuel Akubueze Egejuru and Ketu H. Katrak.

7. The Women Writing Africa project under the direction of Abena Busia and Tuzyline Allen and the Feminist Encyclopedia of African Writing project under the general editorship of Fahamisha Patricia Brown are two examples. To these initiatives I could add the Schomburg Library Nineteenth-Century Black Women Writers, which has already published texts.

8. Three of Virginie Sampeur's poems and five by Ida Faubert were included in Louis Morpeau's 1925 anthology of Haitian poetry covering the years 1817–1925.

9. For a complete discussion of Marie-Magdeleine Carbet's life and work, see E. Anthony Hurley, "Choosing Her Own Name, Or Who Is Carbet?"

10. Marie-Sophie Laborieux, the narrator in Chamoiseau's *Texaco*, is one notable exception.

11. Roger D. Abrahams, *The Man-of-Words in the West Indies and the Emergence of Creole Culture,* and Amadou Hampaté Bâ, "The Living Tradition," in *General History of Africa: Methodology and African Prehistory,* ed. J. Ki-Zerbo, 166–203, devote little space to women's orality.

12. *Fearless Girls, Wise Women, and Beloved Sisters: Heroines in Folktales from around the World,* edited by Kathleen Ragan, is a recent collection on that theme.

13. The plethora of recent studies should not overshadow their predecessors. Because Caribbean women's literature has a longer history than that of its African counterparts, there exist studies on groups as well as individual writers: Maryse Condé's *La Parole des femmes: Essai sur des romancières des Antilles de langue française* (1979); Madeleine Gardiner's *Visages de femmes, portraits d'écrivains* (1981) on Haitian women writers; and Fanta Toureh, *L'imaginaire dans l'oeuvre de Simone Schwarz-Bart: Approche d'une mythologie antillaise* (1986); Roger Toumson, *Pluie et vent sur Télumée Miracle de Simone Schwarz-Bart* (1979).

14. The *New York Times Book Review* has shown an increasing interest in francophone Caribbean literature in the past few years. Not only did it review Lilas Desquiron's novel in May 1998, but it also devoted a 1997 cover article, a rave, to Patrick Chamoiseau's *Texaco.*

Chapter 1

1. Silence is not always stigmatized. For example, enduring in silence the pains of childbirth is a signifier of courage, dignity, and honor in Africa. See Kéita, *Femme d'Afrique,* 261–62. Obioma Nnaemeka posits that one must distinguish between imposed silence and choosing silence, an act of agency which many African women characters do ("Introduction" 4).

2. Angélique Kidjo includes a lullaby to her daughter Naima on her album *Fifa.*

3. See Okpewho, *African Oral Literature,* and Ndiaye, *La Place des femmes.*

4. I am borrowing this concept from Clémentine Faïk-Nzuji in *Symboles graphiques en Afrique,* who concludes that signs that are traced, sculpted, encrusted, drawn, engraved, scarified, painted, tattooed, or woven (61) are important in oral societies, and Edouard Glissant, who considers Haitian painting an oral sign (*Caribbean Discourse* 155–57).

5. Margaret Courtney-Clarke suggests the idea of a book when she writes "lexicon of descriptive images and design formulas" (70). An exhibition consisting of selections from the private collection at the Newark Museum in New Jersey was called "The Language of Cloth: Sub-Saharan African Textiles."

6. See Kathleen Ragan, *Fearless Girls, Wise Women, and Beloved Sisters,* which takes the opposite stance.

7. In Mansour Sora Wade's filmed version of "Fari l'ânesse" (1989), the man who searches for physical perfection in a wife and marries a beautiful stranger is at the center of the tale. The lesson emphasized in this version is that there are more important qualities in a woman than her physical appearance.

8. Numerous studies confirm this fact: See Francesca Velayoudom Faithful, "La femme antillaise"; Claudie Beauvue-Fougeyrollas, *Les femmes antillaises;* France Alibar and Pierrette Lembeye-Boy, *Le couteau seul . . . : La condition féminine aux Antilles;* Germaine Louilot and Danielle Crusol-Baillard, *Femme martiniquaise: Mythe et réalités* (Martinique); Julie Lirus, *Identité antillaise.*

9. Maryse Condé mentions a similar story involving Ti-Jean, who rescues his sister from marrying a devil in disguise; but Ti-Jean is at the center of the story, not his sister. See *La civilisation du bossale: Réflexions sur la littérature orale de la Guadeloupe et de la Martinique,* 143–44.

10. See "Soleil, lune étoile" and "Laurent Palmier" in *Contes et légendes d'Haïti.*

Chapter 2

1. Within the past few years numerous studies have been done in this area. See V. Y. Mudimbe, *The Invention of Africa: Gnosis, Philosophy, and the Order of Knowledge; Parables and Fables: Exegesis, Textuality, and Politics in Central Africa; The Idea of Africa;* Jan Nederveen Pieterse's *White on Black: Images of Africa and Blacks in Western Popular Culture* focuses on men represented in film, children's books, comic books, fiction, and advertising. Raymond Bachollet et al., *Negripub: L'image des Noirs dans la publicité,* examines hundreds of examples of French advertising in which blacks are exploited. Laënnec Hurbon's *Le barbare imaginaire* examines the opposition of "barbarian and civilized" as it relates to Haiti. He does not, however, devote much time to the representation of women. Allison Blakely limits her study to a specific area: *Blacks in the Dutch World: The Evolution of Racial Imagery in a Modern Society.* For a full discussion of scientific racism, see William Cohen, *The French Encounter with Africans: White Response to Blacks, 1530–1880.*

2. Myths about female animality and sexuality in the French *imaginaire* were also contained in the writings of George-Louis Leclerc Buffon, Abbé Raynal, and J. J. Virey; see Sander K. Gilman, *Difference and Pathology: Stereotypes of Sexuality, Race, and Madness.* See also Gilman's "Black Bodies: Towards an Iconography of Female Sexuality in Late Nineteenth Century Art, Medicine, and Literature." On scientific racism, see Cohen (239–41). For a study of the myths surrounding women from the British colonies, see chapter 2, "'The Eye of the Beholder': Contemporary European Images of Black Women," in Barbara Bush, *Slave Women in Caribbean Society, 1650–1838,* 11–22. For a discussion of African American women, see chapter 4, "Mammies, Matriarchs and Other Controlling Images," in Patricia Hill Collins, *Black Feminist Thought: Knowledge, Consciousness, and the Politics of Empowerment,* 67–90. In *White on Black,* Jan Nederveen Pieterse theorizes that physical distance accounts for the differences between the representation of African and African American women in Europe and in the United States. In America, due to the close proximity of slaves and owners, the black woman could be represented as a sexless "mammy." Because European colonialism was in Africa, separating the slaves and owners, the black woman was deemed nonthreatening and figured as a sexpot.

3. See Bryan Hammond's *Josephine Baker,* a compilation of photographs and posters.

4. See Raymond Bachollet et al., *Negripub,* an updated and expanded version of *Negripub: L'image des Noirs dans la publicité depuis un siècle* (Paris: Bibliothèque Forney, 1987), the program from the museum exhibition. *Negripub* is divided into sections: the image of blacks in caricature, travel writings, poster art, and packaging. The famous "Banania" campaign is given its own section. Pascal Blanchard and Armelle Chatelier, ed., *Images et colonies,* gathers the papers from a 1993 conference on the diffusion of colonial ideology through film, painting, advertising, text books, political and military posters, postcards, and newspaper photographs; See also Nicolas Bancel et al., *Images et colonies,* and Yvonne Knibiehler and Régine Goutalier, *La femme au temps des colonies,* which contains thirty- two pages of images of European and African women.

5. Benoist's portrait has become very popular, appearing also on Catherine Hermary-Vieille's novel *L'ange noir,* the Modern Language Association edition of *Ourika,* but without the exposed breast, as it does on the hard- and soft-cover American translations of Patrick Chamoiseau's novel *Texaco.* Robert Deville and Nicolas Georges borrow Benoist's portrait for the cover of their *Les Départements d'outre mer, l'autre décolonisation;* the woman's headscarf is red, white, and blue.

6. Aimé Césaire protests against these stereotypical images of women in his *Cahier d'un retour au pays natal:*

> on voit encore des madras aux reins des femmes des
> anneaux à leurs oreilles des sourires à leurs bouches
> des enfants à leurs mamelles et j'en passe:
> ASSEZ DE CE SCANDALE! (32)

> Women are still seen with madras cloth
> round their loins rings in their ears
> smiles on their mouths babies
> at their breast and all the rest of it:
> ENOUGH OF THIS OUTRAGE! (61)

7. See Bachollet et al., *Negripub.*

8. To all of these representations we can add the emaciated body of the African woman, victim of famine, disease, and drought that is prevalent on the news today.

9. Léon-François Hoffmann, *Le nègre romantique: Personnage littéraire et obsession collective;* Léon Fanoudh-Siefer, *Le mythe du nègre et de l'Afrique noire dans la littérature française de 1800 à la deuxième guerre mondiale;* Ada Martinkus-Zemp, *Le Blanc et le noir: Essai d'une description de la vision du Noir par le Blanc dans la littérature française de l'entre-deux-guerres;* Joachim Sebastien, *Le nègre dans le roman blanc;* Christopher L. Miller, *Blank Darkness: Africanist Discourse in French;* see also Marc Christophe, "Changing Images of Blacks in Eighteenth Century French Literature." The Haitian woman is referred to as a wench in novels of the American occupation, such as William Seabrooks's *Magic Island* (1929) and Irwin Franklyn's *Knights of the Cockpit: A Romantic Epic of the*

Flying Marines in Haiti (1931). She is also associated with Voodoo, not the bona fide religion, but the stereotyped paradigm of witches, zombies, animal sacrifices, cannibalism, and curses.

10. The parallel to the advertisement for Tropic punch and the way in which Janet Museveni is photographed in the 1990s is striking.

11. Hoffmann, *Le nègre romantique*, 223–27.

12. See Annette Kuhn, *The Power of the Image: Essays on Representation and Sexuality;* Ruth Frankenberg, *White Women, Race Matters: The Social Construction of Whiteness;* and Robin Lakoff and Raquel L. Scherr, *Face Value: The Politics of Beauty.*

13. According to Serer belief, the moon does not shine as brightly as the sun because "the moon muted her own light so that her daughter might watch, without being blinded, her mother the moon bathing naked." Robin Morgan, ed., *Sisterhood Is Global,* 593.

14. Diakhaté quoted in Pierrette Herzberger-Fofana, *Ecrivains africains et identités culturelles,* 66–67.

15. For a discussion of the mother figure in twenty novels by male writers see Alphamoye Sonfo, "La mère dans la littérature romanesque de la Guinée, du Mali et du Sénégal." For a discussion on the mother/son relationship in African American literature, see Fritz H. Pointer, "Laye, Lamming and Wright: Mother and Son."

16. See Richard Bjornson, *The African Quest for Freedom and Identity: Cameroonian Writing and the National Experience,* 315. See also Kembe Milolo's discussion in *L'image de la femme chez les romancières de l'Afrique noire francophone.*

17. Sembène's women characters are the object of many studies: Renée Linkhorn, "L'Afrique de demain: Femmes en marche dans l'oeuvre de Sembène Ousmane," 69–76; Ronnie Scharfman, "Fonction romanesque féminine: Rencontre de la culture et de la structure dans *Les bouts de bois de Dieu.*"

18. For a discussion on who is responsible for her death, see Kandioura Dramé, *The Novel as Transformation Myth: A Study of the Novels of Mongo Beti and Ngugi wa Thiong'o,* 56–67.

19. Women also frame Sembène's *L'Harmattan;* chapter 1 opens on midwife Manh Kombéti and closes on Tioumbé.

20. For a discussion of Henri Lopès's female characters, see Anne Adams Graves, "The Works of Henri Lopès: A Forum for African Women's Consciousness," *Ngambika,* 131–38.

21. Edouard Glissant, *Caribbean Discourse: Selected Essays,* 105, 129–31.

22. For a discussion of the significance of M'man Tine's hands, see Eileen Julien, "Métamorphose du réel dans *La rue cases-nègres.*" I agree with her conclusion that this text is a "récit d'héroïsme, mais d'héroïsme féminin" (a narrative of heroism, but of female heroism) because of the sacrifices of M'man Tine.

23. André Ntonfo discerns Zobel's sympathy for these women in the names he chooses for their characters: "Zobel cherche une certaine douceur en nommant ses femmes—leurs noms terminent en 'ie,' 'ine' ou 'ise'" (Zobel searches for a certain

sweetness in naming his women: their names end in "ie," "ine" or "ise"), *L'homme et l'identité dans le roman des Antilles et Guyane françaises*, 51.

24. In the film version by Euzhan Palcy, Adréa works in the box office of a movie theater that has just been robbed. She makes a similar condemnation by distancing herself from all blacks and expresses a desire to be white.

25. Léon-François Hoffmann, "L'image de la femme dans la poésie haïtienne"; Robert Manuel, *La lutte des femmes dans les romans de Jacques-Stéphen Alexis*; Régine Altagrâce Latortue, "In Search of Women's Voice: The Woman Novelist in Haiti," divides women characters into two categories, the angel and the beast (181–94); Gérard Etienne, *La femme noire dans le discours littéraire haïtien*; Max Dorsinville, "Violence et représentation féminine dans le roman haïtien," in *La Deriva delle francofonie: Figures et fantasmes de la violence dans les littératures francophones de l'Afrique subsaharienne et des Antilles*, 2:63–78.

26. Senghor does not completely ignore women as the object of his desire. The second stanza of "Femme noire" reads:

Femme nue, femme obscure
Fruit mûr à la chair ferme, sombres extases du vin noir, bouche qui fais
     lyrique ma bouche
Savane aux horizons purs, savane qui frémis aux caresses ferventes du
     Vent d'Est
Tamtam sculpté, tamtam tendu qui grondes sous les doigts du vainqueur
Ta voix grave de contralto est le chant spirituel de l'Aimée. (270–71)

(Naked woman, dark woman
Ripe fruit with firm flesh, dark raptures of black wine,
Mouth that gives music to my mouth
Savanna of clear horizons, savanna quivering to the fervent caress
Of the East Wind, sculptured tom-tom, stretched drumskin
Moaning under the hands of the conqueror
Your deep contralto voice is the spiritual song of the Beloved.) (8–9)

David Diop's poem "Rama Kam" (an anagram of Virginie Kamara, Diop's first wife) reveals a similar eroticized female.

27. Dépestre's collection of short stories *Eros dans un train chinois* (1990) contains a glossary of terms designating female and male sex organs.

28. It is interesting to note that the roles of M'man Tine and Délira were both played by Darling Légitimus in the Euzhan Palcy movie *Rue cases-nègres* and Benjamin Jules-Rosette's touring stage adaptation of *Gouverneurs de la rosée*, in which she won an award at the Venice Theater Festival.

29. See Robert Manuel, *La lutte des femmes dans les romans de Jacques-Stéphen Alexis*.

Chapter 3

1. "By voicelessness we mean the historical absence of the woman writer's text: the absence of a specifically female position on major issues such as slavery, colo-

nialism, decolonization, women's rights and more direct social and cultural issues." Carole Boyce Davies and Elaine Savory Fido, "Introduction: Women and Literature in the Caribbean: An Overview," *Out of the Kumbla: Women and Literature in the Caribbean,* 1. Davies expands the concept of voicelessness to include the refusal to hear in "Hearing Black Women's Voices: Transgressing Imposed Boundaries," *Moving Beyond Boundaries,* 1:3–14.

2. Cheryl Wall derives her title from Zora Neale Hurston; Irène Assiba d'Almeida borrows the notion of "destroying the emptiness of silence" from Calixthe Beyala. We could also add to the list the autobiography by Sarah L. Delany and A. Elizabeth Delany with Amy Hill Hearth, *Having Our Say: The Delany Sisters' First Hundred Years.* Awa Thiam's work was translated into English as *Speak Out, Black Sisters.*

3. See especially Irele, Julien, Dehon, Laroche, Okpewho, Koné, Glissant.

4. When *Ton beau capitaine* was staged at Brown University, the director, George Houston Bass, chose to have the character Marie-Ange appear on stage. Schwarz-Bart, who was in attendance, was displeased, to say the least.

5. Francophone African and Caribbean women writers are not unique in their desire to reconnect women's orature and literature in a postcolonial context. Contemporary women writers of the non-francophone African diaspora recognize the link between older women's talk and their own coming to writing. See Ogunyemi for Nigerian literature. Paule Marshall is one such appreciative heir, labeling "bards" those women who would congregate in her mother's kitchen after a long and tedious day's work and discuss current events. To the young Paule, these were precious moments "in the wordshop." Marshall appropriately borrows from the language of education when she writes that she "graduated" from the corner of the kitchen to the neighborhood library, and thus from the spoken to the written word (9). Although "graduated" implies an ascension, a hierarchy, the reader should not infer that Marshall stigmatizes orature. Alice Walker is another writer who acknowledges the influence of the woman's oral tradition, in particular that of her mother: "I have absorbed not only the stories themselves, but something of the manner in which she spoke, something of the urgency that involves the knowledge that her stories—like her life—must be recorded" (240). Nourbese Philip admits to "trying to find . . . the deep structures of that oral language" in her work (19). Toni Morrison hints at a call-and-response strategy when she writes of her quest "to construct the dialogue so that it is heard" (341).

6. *Je suis martiniquaise* is often miscategorized as an autobiography. Recently uncovered information reveals otherwise. See Beatrice Stitch Clark, "Who Was Mayotte Capécia? An Update."

7. Republished as *En attendant le bonheur.*

8. For a discussion of other rituals—such as the onguda and mevungu among Beti women—see Jeanne-Françoise Vincent, *Traditions et transition: Entretiens avec des femmes Beti du Sud-Cameroun* and Jean-Claude Barbier, ed., *Femmes du Cameroun: Mères pacifiques, femmes rebelles.* In Senegal, *njam*—the women's tattooing ceremony—is another site of women's culture.

9. See also Aoua Kéita's autobiography, *La vie d'Aoua Kéita racontée par elle-même,* in which she recalls her mother's stories about what happens to a rebellious girl who wants to choose her own husband.

10. Actually when Victoire meets a new man, she leaves daughter Télumée with her mother, Toussine, to raise.

11. For example, Télumée says: "Nous (les Lougandor) connaissons la victoire et les yeux crevés" (We know victory and eyes gouged out) (121/115); "et ma victoire, la preuve que le nègre a sept fiels et ne désarme pas comme ça, à la première alerte" (and my victory the proof that a Negro has seven spleens and doesn't give up just like that at the first sign of trouble) (169/164); "je n'y avais pas vu ma victoire de négresse, ni ma victoire de femme" (I hadn't realized the victory I'd won, as a Negress and as a woman) (112/106).

12. This episode repeats what happened to Télumée's father Angebert, who had befriended Germain, who later killed him.

13. For a discussion on *soukounyan,* a person with special powers to harm, see Dany Bébel-Gisler, *Léonora,* 304.

14. Grandmother Toussine also undergoes a similar experience. Falling into a deep depression after the death of her ten-year-old daughter, Méranée, it is three years before she recovers, to the delight of her neighbors who crown her Reine Sans Nom, or Queen Without a Name, for her rare courage, a quality she had inherited from her mother, Minerve: "elle possédait une foi inébranlable en la vie" (She had an unshakable faith in life) (13/5).

15. Edouard Glissant makes the same assertion that in the Caribbean time is not measured by the calendar (1989). Dany Bébel-Gisler explains that 1848 and 1946 marked administrative changes only which did not alter the colonial system (*Le défi culturel guadeloupéen* 97).

16. Dany Bébel-Gisler describes this important form of resistance during slavery in *Le défi culturel guadeloupéen,* 157.

17. The Bray translation—"triggered off his drum" (206)—does not capture the idea of printing, engraving.

18. The Bray translation omits "en détachant ses mots," which is central to the concept of printing, engraving, which echoes Adiaffi's trope of the drummer in *La carte d'identité.*

19. See Schwarz-Bart, "Sur les pas," 16.

Chapter 4

1. Maryse Condé is more cynical: In *La vie scélérate* (Tree of Life) she writes: "L'amitié entre femmes peut ressembler à l'amour. Elle en a la possessivité, les jalousies, les abandons. Mais sa complicité est plus durable, car elle ne s'appuie pas sur le langage des corps" (Friendship between women can resemble love. It has the same possessiveness as love, the same jealousies and lack of restraint. But the complicities of friendship are more durable than those of love, for they are not based on the language of the body) (206/212). And yet in the text, Thécla and Ottavia are close friends despite nationality and class differences.

2. Women writers seem to be positive about the possibility of female interracial friendship. In Maryse Condé's *Moi, Tituba sorcière* both Tituba and Hester are accused of witchcraft, banished by Puritan society, and brought together by circumstance. In Calixthe Beyala's *Tu t'appelleras Tanga* Cameroonian Tanga relates her life story to French and Jewish Anna-Claude, her cellmate. Young Coco is friends with white Jamaican Melissa in Maryse Condé's *La vie scélérate*. In spite of racial differences the friendship prevails.

3. Chamoiseau and Confiant have also suggested a comparison between slavery and the Holocaust, referring to slavery as the holocaust of holocausts (*Lettres créoles* 31).

4. The message in "Petit mari" (Little husband) is that mother and daughters are rivals, too.

Chapter 5

1. See especially Mongo Beti, "Affaire Calixthe Beyala: Mongo Beti dénonce et accuse," 6–8. I am grateful to Marie-Noëlle Bilong for bringing this article to my attention.

2. There are two embedded tales in *C'est le soleil,* one borrowed from the Bible and the other, related in the text, explaining women's origins on earth and their relationship with men.

3. Beyala has said that an editor, not she, chose the title.

4. Beyala valorizes the particular kind of women's silence that speaks volumes, dedicating her 1994 novel—*L'Asseze, L'Africaine*—to "Asseze S., toi la Femme dont le silence a su si bien me parler" (to Asseze, you, the Woman whose silence knew how to speak to me so well). As in *L'étoile noire,* women's silence here is reconfigured as "articulate."

5. For a report on the December 1988, UNESCO-organized meeting in Brazzaville on the causes of prostitution, see Crépin Bitoumbou.

6. See especially Micheline Labelle and David Nicholls.

7. According to Fanon, the colonized are spectators to their own denigration. See especially chapter 6 in *Peau noire, masques blancs* and to a lesser degree *Les damnés de la terre*. It is not until the close of *Amour* that Claire achieves the status of Fanon's privileged actor. *C'est le soleil* opens on a similar note: "Ici, il y a un creux, il y a le vide, il y a le drame" (Here, there is a hollow, there is emptiness, there is tragedy) (11/1).

8. For more precise details, see the Erma Saint-Grégoire interview in *Callaloo*. See also Carrol F. Coates, "Three Fictional Views of Duvalierist Haiti."

9. Calédu is aptly named, as Régine Latortue points out Calédu in Creole means "one who beats hard" (*calé* = to beat, du = hard) in "In Search of Women's Voices: The Woman Novelist in Haiti" (192).

10. Pedro Sandin-Fremaint defines three spaces in the novel: Claire, the *marrons,* and the public, in *A Theological Reading of Four Novels by Marie Chauvet: In Search of Christic Voices.*

11. Laetitia in *Clémentine,* by Sonia Catalan, has a similar goal: "(elle) tenait

des cahiers où elle consignait des maximes, sentences, observations. On y trouvait des réflexions sur la littérature, la philosophie, l'art, la musique, la politique, le folklore, sur la simplicité des comportements masculins en contraste avec les subtilités des conduites féminines" ([Laetitia] kept notebooks where she wrote maxims, sayings, observations. One could find reflections on literature, philosophy, art, music, politics, folklore, on the simplicity of masculine behaviors in contrast with the subtleties of feminine behaviors) (103).

12. Vèvè Clark notes that Maryse Condé's *Hérémakhonon* is a revision of *Amour* in its "portrayal of the protagonist's sexual behavior as a strategy for drawing the reader into the political repression concealed in the narrative" (46).

Chapter 6

1. Perhaps the large number of articles in this issue on women autobiographers could be ascribed to the fact that eight out of the nine contributors are women. On the other hand, of the fourteen essays in Janos Riesz and Ulla Schild, eds. *Genres autobiographiques en Afrique* (Autobiographical Genres in Africa), only one is centered on women: Bodo Ramangason's "Femmes en autobiographies à Madagascar: Figures d'évolution dans l'espace et dans le temps." This volume assembles the papers from a conference in Berlin on African autobiography.

2. Mayotte Capécia's *Je suis martiniquaise* (1948), best known as the target of Frantz Fanon's criticism in *Peau noire, masques blancs,* has been misidentified as autobiography, perhaps because of its first-person narrator.

3. *Yakaré: L'autobiographie d'Oumar,* recounted orally to Renée Colin-Nogues, raises similar questions. Philippe Lejeune addresses this issue as follows: "autobiography composed in collaboration . . . 'division of labor' between two people (at least) reveals the multiplicity of authorities implied in the work of autobiographical writing, as in all writing. Far from imitating the unity of the authentic autobiography, it emphasizes its indirect and calculated character . . . Collaboration blurs in a disturbing way the question of responsibility, and even damages the notion of identity" (see 187–92).

4. The front cover of *Bonsoir, faites de doux rêves* is designed to insist on dignity and difference from stereotypical visual images of black women. Showing a color photograph of Maillet, a fully dressed woman in her early thirties, smiling, wearing makeup, and "sans madras," it functions as a counter image to the commodified Caribbean woman normally pictured on packaging for rum. The text also contains photographs of Maillet's family as well as her with athletes and celebrities such as Sammy Davis Jr. and the Harlem Globetrotters. The last photograph, of two young white fans kissing her cheek, reverses the image in the advertisement for Tropique punch in which a black woman gazes adoring at the foregrounded white woman. By including several pages of Martinican recipes and a glossary of Creole terms, Maillet valorizes her island's culture, thereby wresting it from touristic inscriptions.

5. Elaine Lawless advocates a new approach called "reciprocal ethnography" to acknowledge the exchange that takes place between interviewer and interviewee in

"Women's Life Stories and Reciprocal Ethnography as Feminist and Emergent." Recently published books tend to allow women to speak for themselves: Irene Staunton, ed., *Mothers of the Revolution: The War Experiences of Thirty Zimbabwean Women* is a collection of interviews with women who provide not only their perspectives on the war experience but also other autobiographical information; Shula Marks, ed., *Not Either an Experimental Doll: The Separate Worlds of Three South African Women* through the correspondence of Lily Moya, Sibusisiwe Makhanya, and Mabel Palme provides a record of their lives and the conditions in South Africa during the 1940s and 1950s; Sarah Mirza and Margaret Strobel, eds., *Three Swahili Women: Life Histories from Mombasa, Kenya.*

6. Public silence is also noted among Sarakolé, Peul, and Moorish women by Aoua Kéita, whose tradition deemed that the women not speak aloud in public. Until the 1950s these women could not attend meetings with men and "parler en public à haute voix était sacrilège pour une femme de bonne famille. Même dans un groupement de femmes, elles se servaient toujours de femmes ou d'hommes de caste qui communiquaient leurs pensées à l'assemblée" (speaking in public was sacreligious for a woman from a good family. Even in a group, they always used casted men or women who communicated their thoughts to the group) (297–98).

Conclusion

1. There is also a school in Dakar named after Nafissatou Diallo.

Bibliography

Abrahams, Roger D. *The Man-of-Words in the West Indies and the Emergence of Creole Culture*. Baltimore: John Hopkins University Press, 1983.

Adiaffi, Jean-Marie. *La carte d'identité*. Paris: Hatier, 1980.

Aidoo, Ama Ata. "Literature, Feminism and the African Woman Today." In *Reconstructing Womanhood, Reconstructing Feminism: Writings on Black Women*, ed. Delia Jarrett-Macauley, 156–74. London: Routledge, 1996.

Alexis, Jacques Stéphen. *Compère Général Soleil*. Paris: Gallimard, 1955.

———. *L'espace d'un cillement*. Paris: Gallimard, 1959.

Alibar, France, and Pierrette Lembeye-Boy. *Le couteau seul . . . : La condition féminine aux Antilles*. Paris: Editions Caribéennes, 1981.

Amadiume, Ifi. *Male Daughters, Female Husbands*. London: Zed Books, 1987.

Aumis, Frédéric. "Bijoux et costumes d'apparat." In *Femmes: Livre d'or de la femme créole*, vol. 4, 55–80. Pointe-à-Pitre: Raphy Diffusion, 1988.

Bâ, Amadou Hampaté. "The Living Tradition." In *General History of Africa: Methodology and African Prehistory*, ed. J. Ki-Zerbo, 166–203. London: Heinemann/UNESCO/University of California, Berkeley, 1981.

Bâ, Mariama. "La fonction politique des littératures africaines écrites." *Ecriture française* 3, no. 5 (1981): 4–7.

———. *Un chant écarlate*. Dakar: Nouvelles Editions Africaines, 1981. Trans. Dorothy S. Blair under the title *Scarlet Song* (London: Longman, 1986).

———. *Une si longue lettre*. Dakar: Nouvelles Editions Africaines, 1979. Trans. Modupé Bodé-Thomas under the title *So Long a Letter* (London: Heinemann, 1981).

Bachollet, Raymond, Jean-Barthélémi Devost, Anne-Claude Lelieur, Marie-Christine Peyrière. *Negripub*. Paris: Somogy, 1992.

Baker, Jean-Claude, and Chris Chase. *Josephine Baker: The Hungry Heart*. New York: Random House, 1993.

Baker, Josephine, and Jo Bouillon. *Josephine*. Trans. Mariana Fitzpatrick. New York: Harper and Row, 1977.

Balou-Tchichelle, Jeannette. *Coeur en exil*. Paris: La Pensée Universelle, 1989.

Bancel, Nicolas, Pascal Blanchard, and Laurent Gervereau, eds. *Images et colonies: Iconographie et propagande coloniale sur l'Afrique française de 1880 à 1962*. Paris: L'ACHAC, 1993.

Barbier, Jean-Claude, ed. *Femmes du Cameroun: Mères pacifiques, femmes rebelles*. Paris: Karthala/Orstom, 1985.

Barry, Kesso. *Kesso: Princesse peuhle*. Paris: Seghers, 1988.

Barthélémy, Mimi. *Contes diaboliques d'Haïti*. Paris: Karthala, 1995.

———. *Malice et l'âne qui chie de l'or et autres contes d'Haïti*. Paris: Syros/Fort-de-France, Vent des îles, 1994.

Bascom, William, ed. *African Dilemma Tales*. The Hague/Paris: Mouton, 1975.

Beauvue-Fougeyrollas, Claudie. *Les femmes antillaises*. Paris: L'Harmattan, 1979.

Bébel-Gisler, Dany. *Le défi culturel guadeloupéen: Devenir ce que nous sommes*. Paris: Editions Caribéennes, 1989.

———. *Léonora: L'histoire enfouie de la Guadeloupe*. Paris: Seghers, 1985. Trans. Andrea Leskes under the title *Leonora: The Buried Story of Guadeloupe* (Charlottesville: University Press of Virginia, 1994).

Benitez-Rojo, Antonio. *The Repeating Island: The Caribbean and the Postmodern Perspective*. Trans. James E. Maraniss. Durham: Duke University Press, 1992.

Bernabé, Jean, Patrick Chamoiseau, and Raphaël Confiant. *Eloge de la créolité/In Praise of Creoleness*. Bilingual ed. Trans. Mohamed B. Taleb Khyar. Paris: Gallimard, 1993.

Beti, Mongo. "Affaire Calixthe Beyala: Mongo Beti dénonce et accuse. . . ." *Galaxie* 204 (March 26, 1997): 6–8.

———. *Perpétue et l'habitude du malheur*. Paris: Editions Buchet-Chastel, 1974.

———. *Remember Ruben*. Paris: L'Harmattan, 1982.

Beuze, Lyne-Rose. *Costumes de femmes: Traditions vestimentaires en Martinique de 1870 à 1940*. Fort-de-France: Bureau du Patrimoine du Conseil Régional de la Martinique, 1989.

Beyala, Calixthe. *C'est le soleil qui m'a brûlée*. Paris: Stock, 1987. Trans. Marjolijn de Jager under the title *The Sun Hath Looked Upon Me* (Oxford/Portsmouth, N.H.: Heinemann, 1996).

———. *Les honneurs perdus*. Paris: Albin Michel, 1996.

———. "Interview." *Amina* 223 (November 1988): 85.

———. *Lettre d'une africaine à ses soeurs occidentales*. Paris: Spengler, 1995.

———. *La petite fille du réverbère*. Paris: Albin Michel, 1998.

———. *Seul le diable le savait*. Paris: Le Pré aux Clercs, 1990.

———. *Tu t'appelleras Tanga*. Paris: Stock, 1988.

Bitoumbou, Crépin. "Les Causes de la prostitution étudiées par des experts." *Amina* 227 (March 1989): 64.

Bjornson, Richard. *The African Quest for Freedom and Identity: Cameroonian Writing and the National Experience*. Bloomington: Indiana University Press, 1991.

Blakely, Allison. *Blacks in the Dutch World: The Evolution of Racial Imagery in a Modern Society*. Bloomington: Indiana University Press, 1993.

Blanchard, Pascal, and Armelle Chatelier, eds. *Images et colonies: Nature, discours et influence de l'iconographie coloniale liée à la propagande coloniale et à la représentation des Africains et de l'Afrique en France de 1920 aux indépendances*. Actes du colloque organisé par l'ACHAC du 20 au 22 janvier 1985 à la Bibliothèque Nationale. Paris: Syros, 1993.

Blouin, Andrée, with Jean MacKellar. *My Country, Africa: Autobiography of the Black Pasionaria*. New York: Praeger, 1983.

Borgomano, Madeleine. *Voix et visages de femmes dans les livres écrits par les femmes en Afrique francophone*. Abidjan: CEDA, 1989.

Brière, Eloise A. *Le Roman camerounais et ses discours*. Ivry: Nouvelles du sud, 1993.

Bugul, Ken. *Le baobab fou*. Dakar: Nouvelles Editions Africaines, 1982. Trans. Marjolijn de Jager under the title *The Abandoned Baobab: The Autobiography of a Senegalese Woman* (Brooklyn: Lawrence Hill Books, 1991).

———. *Cendres et braises*. Paris: L'Harmattan, 1994.

Busby, Margaret, ed. *Daughters of Africa: An International Anthology of Words and Writings by Women of African Descent from the Ancient Egyptian to the Present*. New York: Ballantine Books, 1994.

Bush, Barbara. *Slave Women in Caribbean Society, 1650–1838*. Bloomington: Indiana University Press, 1990.

Capécia, Mayotte. *Je suis martiniquaise*. Paris: Editions Corréa, 1948. Trans. Beatrice Stith Clark under the titles *I Am a Martinican Woman* and *The White Negress* (Pueblo, Colo.: Passeggiata, 1997).

Catalan, Sonia. *Clémentine*. Paris: L'Harmattan, 1992.

Cazenave, Odile. *Femmes rebelles: Naissance d'un nouveau roman africain au féminin*. Paris: L'Harmattan, 1996.

Certeau, Michel de. *Heterologies: Discourse on the Other*. Trans. Brian Massumi. Minneapolis: University of Minnesota Press, 1986.

Césaire, Aimé. *Cahier d'un retour au pays natal*. Paris: Présence Africaine, 1983. Trans. John Berger and Anna Bostock under the title *Return to My Native Land* (Middlesex, England: Penguin Books, 1969).

Césaire, Ina. "Conte africain originel et conte antillais résurgent." *Notre Librairie* 73 (1984): 77–85.

———. *Contes de nuits et de jours aux Antilles*. Paris: Editions Caribéennes, 1989.

Chamoiseau, Patrick. *Solibo magnifique*. Paris: Folio, 1991.

———. *Texaco*. Paris: Gallimard, 1992.

Chamoiseau, Patrick, and Raphaël Confiant. *Lettres créoles: Tracées antillaises et continentales de la littérature 1635–1975*. Paris: Hatier, 1991.

Chancy, Miriam J. A. *Framing Silence: Revolutionary Novels by Haitian Women*. New Brunswick: Rutgers University Press, 1997.

Chauvet, Marie. *Amour, colère et folie*. Paris: Gallimard, 1968.

Christophe, Marc. "Changing Images of Blacks in Eighteenth Century French Literature." *Phylon* 48, no. 3 (fall 1987): 183–89.

La civilisation de la femme dans la tradition africaine. Paris: Présence Africaine, 1975.

Cixous, Hélène. "The Laugh of the Medusa." Trans. Keith Cohen and Paul Cohen. In *New French Feminisms*, ed. Elaine Marks and Isabelle de Courtivron, 245–64. New York: Schocken Books, 1981.

Clark, Beatrice Stith. "Who Was Mayotte Capécia? An Update." *CLA Journal* 39, no. 4 (June 1996): 454–57.

Clark, Vèvè A. "Developing Diaspora Literacy and 'Marasa' Consciousness." In *Comparative American Identities: Race, Sex and Nationality in the Modern Text*, ed. Hortense Spillers, 40–61. New York: Routledge, 1991.

Coates, Carrol F. "Three Views of Duvalierist Haiti." In *Haitian Studies Association Second Annual Conference Proceedings June 15–16, 1990*, ed. Vèvè A. Clark and Alix Cantave, 180–92. Medford: Tufts University Press, 1991.

Codere, Helen. *The Biography of an African Society Based on 48 Rwandan Autobiographies, 1900–1960*. Tervuren: Musée Royal de l'Afrique Centrale, 1973.

Cohen, William. *The French Encounter with Africans: White Response to Blacks, 1530–1880*. Bloomington: Indiana University Press, 1980.

Collins, Patricia Hill. *Black Feminist Thought: Knowledge, Consciousness, and the Politics of Empowerment*. Boston: Unwin Hyman, 1990.

Comhaire-Sylvain, Suzanne. *Le roman de Bouqui*. Ottawa: Leméac, 1973.

Condé, Maryse. *La civilisation du bossale: Réflexions sur la littérature orale de la Guadeloupe et de la Martinique*. Paris: L'Harmattan, 1978.

———. *Désirada*. Robert Laffont, 1997.

———. *Hérémakhonon*. Paris: Union Générale d'Editions, 1976.

———. *La migration des coeurs*. Paris: Robert Laffont, 1995.

———. *Moi, Tituba sorcière . . . noire de Salem*. Paris: Livre de Poche, 1986. Trans. Richard Philcox under the title *I, Tituba, Black Witch of Salem* (Charlottesville: University Press of Virginia, 1992).

———. "Order, Disorder, Freedom, and the West Indian Writer." *Yale French Studies* 83 (1993): 121–35.

———. *La parole des femmes: Essai sur des romancières des Antilles de langue française*. Paris: L'Harmattan, 1979.

———. *Ségou: La terre en miettes*. Paris: Robert Laffont, 1985.

———. *Ségou: Les murailles de terre*. Paris: Robert Laffont, 1984.

———. *Traversée de la mangrove*. Paris: Mercure de France, 1989. Trans. Richard Philcox under the title *Crossing the Mangrove* (New York: Doubleday/Anchor Books, 1995).

———. "Trois femmes à Manhattan." *Présence Africaine* 121–22 (1982): 307–15.

———. *Une saison à Rihata*. Paris: Robert Laffont, 1981. Trans. Richard Philcox under the title *A Season in Rihata* (London: Heinemann, 1988).

———. *La vie scélérate*. Paris: Seghers, 1987. Trans. Victoria Reiter under the title *Tree of Life* (New York: Ballantine, 1992).

Confiant, Raphaël. *Les maîtres de la parole créole*. Paris: Gallimard, 1995.

———. *Ravines du devant-jour*. Paris: Gallimard, 1993.

Coquery-Vidrovitch, Catherine. *Les africaines: Histoire des femmes d'Afrique noire du XIXe au XXe siècle*. Paris: Desjonquères, 1994.

Courtney-Clarke, Margaret. *African Canvas: The Art of West African Women*. New York: Rizzoli, 1990.

Dadié, Bernard. *Le pagne noir*. Paris: Présence Africaine, 1955.

d'Almeida, Irène Assiba. *Francophone African Women Writers: Destroying the Emptiness of Silence*. Gainesville: University Press of Florida, 1994.

Danticat, Edwidge. *Breath, Eyes, Memory.* New York: Vintage, 1995.

———. *The Farming of Bones.* New York: Soho, 1998.

———. *Krik? Krak!* New York: Vintage Books, 1996.

Davies, Carole Boyce. *Black Women Writing and Identity: Migrations of the Subject.* London/New York: Routledge, 1994.

———. "Collaboration and the Ordering Imperative in Life Story Production." In *De/Colonizing the Subject: The Politics of Gender in Women's Autobiography,* ed. Sidonie Smith and Julia Watson, 3–19. Minneapolis: University of Minnesota Press, 1992.

———. "Private Selves and Public Spaces: Autobiography and African Woman Writers." *CLA Journal* 34, no. 3 (March 1991): 267–89.

Davies, Carole Boyce, and Elaine Savory Fido, eds. *Out of the Kumbla: Caribbean Women and Literature.* Trenton: Africa World Press, 1990.

Davies, Carole Boyce, and Anne Adams Graves, eds. *Ngambika: Studies of Women in African Literature.* Trenton: Africa World Press, 1986.

Davies, Carole Boyce, and 'Molara Ogundipe-Leslie, eds. *Moving Beyond Boundaries.* Vol. 1. New York: New York University Press, 1995.

Dayan, Joan. "Hallelujah for a Garden Woman: The Caribbean Adam and His Pretext." *French Review* 59, no. 4 (March 1986): 581–95.

———. "Reading Women in the Caribbean: Marie Chauvet's Love, Anger, and Madness." In *Displacements: Women, Tradition, Literatures in French,* ed. Jean Dejean and Nancy K. Miller, 228–53. Baltimore: Johns Hopkins University Press, 1991.

Dehon, Claire. "Les influences du conte traditionnel dans le roman camerounais d'expression française." *Neohelicon* 16, no. 2 (1989): 9–37.

Delany, Sarah L., and A. Elizabeth Delany, with Amy Hill Hearth. *Having Our Say: The Delany Sisters' First Hundred Years.* New York: Kodansha, 1993.

Dépestre, René. "Bref éloge de la langue française." *La quinzaine littéraire* 436 (March 16–31, 1985): 33.

———. *Eros dans un train chinois.* Paris: Gallimard, 1990.

Desquiron, Lilas. *Les chemins de Loco-Miroir.* Paris: Presses Pocket, 1990.

Dia, Oumar, and Renée Colin-Nogues. *Yakaré: L'autobiographie d'Oumar.* Paris: Maspéro/La Découverte, 1982.

Diagne, Rokhaya Oumar, and Souleymane Bachir Diagne. "Annette Mbaye d'Erneville, femme de communication." *Présence Africaine* 153 (1996): 93–97.

Diakhaté, Ndèye Coumba Mbengue. "Entretien." *Mwasi* 96 (December 1980): 37–38.

———. *Filles du soleil.* Dakar: Nouvelles Editions Africaines, 1980.

Diallo, Nafissatou. *De Tilène au Plateau: Une enfance dakaroise.* Dakar: Nouvelles Editions Africaines, 1975.

Diawara, Mamadou. "Women, Servitude and History: The Oral Historical Traditions of Women in Servile Condition in the Kingdom of Jaara (Mali) from the Fifteenth to the Mid-Nineteenth Century." In *Discourse and Its Disguises: The*

Interpretation of African Oral Texts, ed. Karin Barber and P. F. de Moraes Farias, 109–37. Birmingham, England: Centre of West African Studies, 1989.

Diawara, Manthia. *African Cinema: Politics and Culture.* Bloomington: Indiana University Press, 1991.

Diop, Birago. *Les contes d'Amadou Koumba.* Paris: Présence Africaine, 1961. Trans. Dorothy S. Blair under the title *Tales of Amadou Koumba* (London: Oxford University Press, 1966).

———. *Les nouveaux contes d'Amadou Koumba.* Paris: Présence Africaine, 1961.

Djebar, Assia. *L'amour, la fantasia.* Casablanca: EDDIF, 1992. Trans. Dorothy S. Blair under the title *Fantasia, An Algerian Cavalcade* (Portsmouth, N.H.: Heinemann, 1993).

———. *Femmes d'Alger dans leur appartement.* Paris: Des Femmes, 1980. Trans. Marjolijn de Jager under the title *Women of Algiers in Their Apartment* (Charlottesville: University Press of Virginia, 1992).

Doan, Laura L., ed. *Old Maids to Radical Spinsters: Unmarried Women in the Twentieth-Century Novel.* Urbana: University of Illinois Press, 1991.

Dominique, Jan J. *Mémoire d'une amnésique.* Port-au-Prince: Deschamps, 1984.

Domowitz, Susan. "Wearing Proverbs: Anyi Names for Printed Factory Cloth." *African Arts* 25, no. 3 (July 1992): 82–87.

Dooh-Bunya, Lydie. *La brise du jour.* Yaoundé: Editions CLE, 1977.

Dorsinville, Max. "Violence et représentation féminine dans le roman haïtien." In *La Deriva delle francofonie: Figures et fantasmes de la violence dans les littératures francophones de l'Afrique subsaharienne et des Antilles,* ed. Carla Fratta, 2:63–78. Bologna: CLUEB, 1992.

Dramé, Kandioura. *The Novel as Transformation Myth: A Study of the Novels of Mongo Beti and Ngugi wa Thiong'o.* Syracuse: Syracuse University Press, 1990.

Dugast, I. "Autobiographie d'une femme banen." *Bulletin de la société d'études camerounaises* 6 (1944): 83–96.

Duras, Claire de. *Ourika.* New York: MLA Publications, 1994.

Dusseck, Micheline. *Ecos del caribe.* Barcelona: Lumen, 1996.

Ega, Françoise. *Lettres à une noire.* Paris: L'Harmattan, 1978.

———. *Le temps des madras: Récit de la Martinique.* Paris: Editions Maritimes et d'Outre Mer, 1966.

Etienne, Gérard. *La femme noire dans le discours littéraire haïtien: Éléments d'anthroposémiologie.* Montréal/Paris: Balzac-Le Griot Editeur, 1998.

Faik-Nzuji, Clémentine. *Symboles graphiques en Afrique noire.* Paris: Karthala, 1992.

Fanon, Frantz. *Les damnés de la terre.* Paris: F. Maspero, 1968. Trans. Constance Farrington under the title *The Wretched of the Earth* (New York: Grove Press, 1965).

———. *Peau noire, masques blancs.* Paris: Seuil, 1965. Trans. Charles Lam Markmann under the title *Black Skin, White Masks* (New York: Grove Press, 1967).

Fanoudh-Siefer, Léon. *Le mythe du nègre et de l'Afrique noire dans la littérature française de 1800 à la deuxième guerre mondiale.* Paris: Klinsksieck, 1968.

Fauque, Claude, and Otto Wollenweber. *Tissus d'Afrique.* Paris: Editions Syros Alternatives, 1991.

Fignolé, Jean-Claude. *Les possédés de la pleine lune.* Paris: Seuil, 1987.

Foucault, Michel. *Discipline and Punish.* Trans. Alan Sheridan. New York: Pantheon, 1977.

Frankenberg, Ruth. *White Women, Race Matters: The Social Construction of Whiteness.* Minneapolis: University of Minnesota Press, 1993.

Gallimore, Rangira Béatrice. *L'oeuvre romanesque de Calixthe Beyala: Le renouveau de l'écriture féminine en Afrique francophone sub-saharienne.* Paris: L'Harmattan, 1997.

Gardiner, Madeleine. *Visages de femmes, portraits d'écrivains.* Port-au-Prince: Deschamps, 1981.

Gates, Henry Louis. *Figures in Black: Words, Signs and the "Racial" Self.* Oxford: Oxford University Press, 1989.

Gikandi, Simon. *Writing in Limbo: Modernism and Caribbean Literature.* Ithaca: Cornell University Press, 1992.

Gilman, Sander L. "Black Bodies: Towards an Iconography of Female Sexuality in Late Nineteenth Century Art, Medicine, and Literature." *Critical Inquiry* (autumn 1985): 204–42.

———. *Difference and Pathology: Stereotypes of Sexuality, Race, and Madness.* Ithaca: Cornell University Press, 1985.

Gilroy, Paul. *The Black Atlantic: Modernity and Double Consciousness.* Cambridge: Harvard University Press, 1993.

Glissant, Edouard. *Le discours antillais.* Paris: Seuil, 1981. Trans. J. Michael Dash under the title *Caribbean Discourse: Selected Essays* (Charlottesville: University Press of Virginia, 1989).

———. *Poétique de la relation.* Paris: Gallimard, 1990. Trans. Betsy Wing under the title *Poetics of Relation* (Ann Arbor: University of Michigan Press, 1997).

Gorog-Karady, Veronika, and Gérard Meyer. *Images féminines dans les contes africains.* Paris: CILF, 1988.

Graves, Anne Adams. "The Works of Henri Lopès: A Forum for African Women's Consciousness." In *Ngambika: Studies of Women in African Literature,* ed. Carole Boyce Davies and Anne Adams Graves, 131–38. Trenton: Africa World Press, 1986.

Green, Mary Jean. "Simone Schwarz-Bart et la tradition féminine aux Antilles." *Présence francophone* 36 (1990): 130–33.

Gyssels, Kathleen. *'Filles de Solitude': Essai sur l'identité antillaise dans les (auto)biographies de Simone et André Schwarz-Bart.* Paris: L'Harmattan, 1996.

Hale, Thomas A. *Griots and Griottes: Masters of Words and Music.* Bloomington: Indiana University Press, 1999.

Hammond, Bryan. *Josephine Baker.* London: Jonathan Cape, 1988.

Henderson, Mae Gwendolyn. "Speaking in Tongues: Dialogics, Dialectics, and the Black Women's Literary Tradition." In *Changing Our Own Words: Essays on Criticism, Theory, and Writing by Black Women,* ed. Cheryl A. Wall, 16–37. New Brunswick: Rutgers University Press, 1989.

Herzberger-Fofana, Pierrette. *Ecrivains africains et identités culturelles.* Tubingen: Stauffenburg Verlag, 1989.

Hoffmann, Léon-François. "L'image de la femme dans la poésie haïtienne." *Présence Africaine* 34–35 (1960–61): 183–206.

———. *Le nègre romantique: Personnage littéraire et obsession collective.* Paris: Payot, 1973.

hooks, bell. *Black Looks: Race and Representation.* Boston: South End Press, 1992.

———. *Talking Back: Thinking Feminist, Thinking Black.* Boston: South End Press, 1989.

———. *Yearning: Race, Gender, and Cultural Politics.* Boston: South End Press, 1990.

Huannou, Adrien. *La question des littératures nationales en Afrique noire.* Abidjan: CEDA, 1989.

Hurbon, Laënnec. *Le barbare imaginaire.* Paris: Editions du Cerf, 1988.

Hurley, E. Anthony. "Choosing Her Own Name, Or Who Is Carbet?" *CLA Journal* 41, no. 4 (June 1998): 387–404.

Ilboudo, Patrick G. *Les carnets secrets d'une fille de joie.* Ouagadougou: Editions LaMante, 1988.

Irele, Abiola. "The African Imagination." *Research in African Literatures* 21, no. 1 (spring 1990): 49–67.

Irigaray, Luce. *Speculum de l'autre femme.* Paris: Minuit. Trans. Gillian C. Gill under the title *Speculum of the Other Woman* (Ithaca: Cornell University Press, 1985).

Jeanty, Edner A, and O. Carl Brown. *Parol Gran Moun: Haitian Popular Wisdom.* Port-au-Prince: Editions Learning Center, 1976.

Julien, Eileen. *African Novels and the Question of Orality.* Bloomington: Indiana University Press, 1992.

———. "Métamorphose du réel dans *La rue cases-nègres.*" *French Review* 60, no. 6 (May 1986): 781–87.

Kâ, Aminata Maïga. *La voie du salut suivi de Le Miroir de la vie.* Paris: Présence Africaine, 1985.

Kane, Cheikh Hamidou. *L'aventure ambiguë.* Paris: Juillard, 1961. Trans. Katherine Woods under the title *Ambiguous Adventure* (New York: Collier Books, 1969).

Kane, Mohammdou. *Essai sur les contes d'Amadou Coumba.* Dakar: Nouvelles Editions Africaines, 1981.

———. "Le féminisme dans le roman africain de langue française." *Annales de la faculté de lettres et sciences humaines Université de Dakar* 10 (1980): 143–200.

Kazi-Tani, Nora-Alexandra. *Roman africain de langue française au carrefour de l'écrit et de l'oral.* Paris: L'Harmattan, 1995.

Kéita, Aoua. *Femme d'Afrique: La vie d'Aoua Kéita racontée par elle-même.* Paris: Présence Africaine, 1975.

Knibiehler, Yvonne, and Régine Goutalier. *La femme au temps des colonies.* Paris: Stock, 1985.

Koné, Amadou. *Du récit oral au roman: Étude sur les avatars de la tradition héroïque dans le roman africain.* Abidjan: CEDA, 1985.

Koppelman, Susan. Afterword. *Women's Friendships: A Collection of Short Stories.* Norman: University of Oklahoma Press, 1991.

Kourouma, Ahmadou. *Les soleils des indépendances.* Paris: Seuil, 1970.

Kuhn, Annette. *The Power of the Image: Essays on Representation and Sexuality.* London: Routledge and Kegan Paul, 1985.

Labelle, Micheline. *Idéologie de couleur et classes sociales en Haïti.* Montreal: Les Presses de l'Université de Montréal, 1978.

Labou Tansi, Sony. *L'anté-peuple.* Paris: Seuil, 1983.

Laferrière, Dany. *L'odeur du café: Récit.* Montreal: VLB, 1991.

Lakoff, Robin Tolmach, and Raquel L. Scherr. *Face Value: The Politics of Beauty.* Boston: Routledge and Kegan Paul, 1984.

Laroche, Maximilien. *La double scène de la représentation: Oraliture et littérature dans la Caraïbe.* Quebec: Université Laval/GRELCA, 1991.

Larrier, Renée. "Correspondance et création littéraire: Mariama Bâ's *Une si longue lettre.*" *French Review* 64, no. 5 (April 1991): 747–53.

———. "Les femmes-poètes du Sénégal." *Présence francophone* 36 (1990): 45–56.

———. "Inscriptions of Orality and Silence: Representations of Female Friendship in Francophone Africa and the Caribbean." In *Communication and Women's Friendships: Parallels and Intersections in Literature and Life,* ed. Janet Doubler Ward and Joanna Stephens Mink, 181–94. Bowling Green: Bowling Green State University Popular Press, 1993.

Latortue, Régine Altagrâce. "In Search of Women's Voice: The Woman Novelist in Haiti." In *Wild Women in the Worldwind: Afra-American Culture and the Contemporary Literary Renaissance,* ed. Joanne M. Braxton and Andrée Nicola McLaughlin, 181–94. New Brunswick, N.J.: Rutgers University Press, 1990.

Laurent, Joëlle, and Ina Césaire. *Contes de mort et de vie aux Antilles.* Paris: Editions Caribéennes, 1976.

Laurentin, Anne. "Nzakara Women (Central African Republic)." In *Women of Tropical Africa,* ed. Denise Paulme, 121–78. Trans. H. M. Wright. Berkeley: University of California Press, 1963.

Lawless, Elaine. "Women's Life Stories and Reciprocal Ethnography as Feminist and Emergent." *Journal of Folklore Research* 28, no. 1 (January–April 1991): 35–60.

Laye, Camara. *L'enfant noir.* Paris: Plon, 1953.

Lee, Sonia. "Image of the Woman in the African Folktale from the Sub-Saharan Francophone Area." *Yale French Studies* 53 (1976): 19–28.

Lejeune, Philippe. *On Autobiography.* Trans. Katherine Leary. Minneapolis: University of Minnesota Press, 1989.

Lelieur, Anne-Claude, and Bernard Mirabel, eds. *Negripub: L'image des Noirs dans la publicité depuis un siècle.* Paris: Bibliothèque Forney, 1987.

Lequeret, Elizabeth. "Michèle Maillet, une martiniquaise tout feu, tout femme." *Afrique Magazine* 75 (1990): 17.

Liking, Werewere. *Elle sera de jaspe et de corail.* Paris: L'Harmattan, 1983.

Liking, Werewere, and Marie-José Hourantier. *Contes d'initiation féminine du pays Bassa.* Paris: Editions Saint-Paul, 1981.

Linkhorn, Renée. "L'Afrique de demain: Femmes en marche dans l'oeuvre de Sembène Ousmane." *Modern Language Studies* 16, no. 3 (summer 1986): 69–76.

Lionnet, Françoise. *Autobiographical Voices: Race, Gender, Self-Portraiture.* Ithaca: Cornell University Press, 1989.

Lirus, Julie. *Identité antillaise.* Paris: Editions Caribéennes, 1979.

Lopès, Henri. *La nouvelle romance.* Yaoundé: Editions CLE, 1976.

———. *Le lys et le flamboyant.* Paris: Seuil, 1997.

Louilot, Germaine, and Danielle Crusol-Baillard. *Femme martiniquaise: Mythes et réalités.* Martinique: Desormeaux, 1986.

Magnier, Bernard. "Ken Bugul ou l'écriture thérapeutique." *Notre Librairie* 81 (October–December 1985): 151–55.

Maillet, Michèle. *Bonsoir, faites de doux rêves! Antillaise, speakerine . . . et remerciée!* Paris: Editions Pierre-Marcel Faure, 1982.

———. *L'étoile noire.* Paris: François Bourin, 1990.

Makouta-Mboukou, J. P. *Introduction à l'étude du roman négro- africain de langue française.* Dakar: Nouvelles Editions Africaines, 1980.

Manicom, Jacqueline. *La graine: Journal d'une sage-femme.* Paris: Presse de la Cité, 1974.

Manuel, Robert. *La lutte des femmes dans les romans de Jacques- Stéphen Alexis.* Port-au-Prince: Henri Deschamps, 1980.

Maria, Odet. *Une enfance antillaise: Voyage au fond de ma mémoire.* Paris: L'Harmattan, 1992.

Marks, Shula, ed. *Not Either an Experimental Doll: The Separate Worlds of Three South African Women.* Bloomington: Indiana University Press, 1987.

Marshall, Paule. "The Making of a Writer." In *Reena and Other Stories,* 3–12. Old Westbury, N.Y.: Feminist Press, 1983.

Matateyou, Emmanuel. "Calixthe Beyala: Entre le terroir et l'exil." *French Review* 69, no. 4 (March 1996): 605–15.

———. "Poésie orale traditionnelle et expression du quotidien en Afrique noire." *Francographies* 2 (1995): 57–79.

Mayes, Janis A. "Mind-Body-Soul: Erzulie Embodied in Marie Chauvet's *Amour.*" *Journal of Caribbean Studies* 7, no. 1 (spring 1989): 81–89.

Miller, Christopher L. *Blank Darkness: Africanist Discourse in French.* Chicago: University of Chicago Press, 1985.

————. *Theories of Africans: Francophone Literature and Anthropology in Africa.* Chicago: University of Chicago Press, 1990.

Milolo, Kembe. *L'image de la femme chez les romancières de l'Afrique noire francophone.* Fribourg: Editions Universitaires, 1986.

Mirza, Sarah, and Margaret Strobel, eds. *Three Swahili Women: Life Stories from Mombasa, Kenya.* Bloomington: Indiana University Press, 1989.

Mohanty, Chandra. "Under Western Eyes: Feminist Scholarship and Colonial Discourses." *Feminist Review* 30 (autumn 1988): 65–88.

Mohanty, Chandra Talpade, Anno Russo, and Lourdes Torres, eds. *Third World Women and the Politics of Feminism.* Bloomington: Indiana University Press, 1991.

Morgan, Robin, ed. *Sisterhood Is Global.* Garden City: Anchor Books/Doubleday, 1984.

Morpeau, Louis, ed. *Anthologie d'un siècle de poésie haïtienne, 1817–1925.* Paris: Bossard, 1925.

Morrison, Toni. "'Rootedness': The Ancestor as Foundation." In *Black Women Writers (1950–1980),* ed. Mari Evans, 339–45. New York: Anchor Books, 1984.

Mortimer, Mildred. *Journeys through the French African Novel.* Portsmouth, N.H.: Heinemann, 1990.

Mudimbe, Elizabeth, ed. *Post-Colonial Women's Writing.* Special issue of *L'esprit créateur* 33, no. 2 (summer 1993): 1–136.

Mudimbe, V. Y. *Le bel immonde.* Paris: Présence Africaine, 1976. Trans. Marjolijn de Jager under the title *Before the Birth of the Moon* (New York: Simon and Schuster, 1989).

————. *The Idea of Africa.* Bloomington: Indiana University Press, 1994.

————. *The Invention of Africa: Gnosis, Philosophy, and the Order of Knowledge.* Bloomington: Indiana University Press, 1988.

————. *Parables and Fables: Exegesis, Textuality, and Politics in Central Africa.* Madison: University of Wisconsin Press, 1991.

Nasta, Susheila, ed. *Motherlands: Black Women's Writing from Africa, the Caribbean, and South Asia.* New Brunswick: Rutgers University Press, 1991.

Ndao, Cheik Aliou. *Excellence, vos épouses!* Dakar: Nouvelles Editions Africaines, 1983.

Ndiaye, A. Raphaël. *La place des femmes dans les rites du Sénégal.* Dakar: Nouvelles Editions Africaines, 1986.

Ndione, Ch. Ah. Tidiane. "'Woyi Céét': Traditional Marriage Songs of the Lebu." *Research in African Literatures* 24, no. 2 (summer 1993): 89–100.

Nfah-Abbenyi, Juliana Makuchi. *Gender in African Women's Writing: Identity, Sexuality, and Difference.* Bloomington: Indiana University Press, 1997.

Ngugi wa Thiongo. *Decolonising the Mind.* Portsmouth, N.H.: Heinemann, 1992.

Niane, Djibril Tamsir. *Soundjata ou l'épopée mandingue.* Paris: Présence Africaine, 1960.

Nicholls, David. *From Dessalines to Duvalier: Race, Colour, and National Independence in Haiti.* Cambridge: Cambridge University Press, 1979.

Nnaemeka, Obioma. "Introduction: Imag(in)ing Knowledge, Power, and Subversion in the Margins." In *The Politics of (M)Othering: Womanhood, Identity, and Resistance in African Literature,* ed. Obioma Nnaemeka, 1–25. Routledge: London/New York, 1997.

———. "Mariama Bâ: Parallels, Convergence, and Interior Space." *Feminist Issues* 10, no. 1 (spring 1990): 13–35.

Ntonfo, André. *L'Homme et l'identité dans le roman des Antilles et Guyane françaises.* Sherbrooke: Naaman, 1982.

O'Callaghan, Evelyn. *Woman Version: Theoretical Approaches to West Indian Fiction by Women.* New York: St. Martin's Press, 1993.

L'oeuvre de Maryse Condé: Questions et réponses à propos d'une écrivaine politiquement incorrecte. Actes du colloque international sur l'oeuvre de Maryse Condé, 14–18 mars 1995. Paris: L'Harmattan, 1996.

Ogunyemi, Chikwenye Okonjo. *Africa Wo/Man Palava: The Nigerian Novel by Women.* Chicago: University of Chicago Press, 1996.

Okpewho, Isidore. *African Oral Literature: Backgrounds, Character and Continuity.* Bloomington: Indiana University Press, 1992.

Ong, Walter. *Orality and Literacy: The Technologizing of the Word.* London: Methuen, 1982.

Oyono, Ferdinand. *Le vieux nègre et la médaille.* Paris: 10/18, 1986.

Paulme, Denise. *La mère dévorante: Essai sur la morphologie des contes africains.* Paris: Gallimard, 1976.

Pépin, Ernest. "La Femme antillaise et son corps." *Présence Africaine* 14 (1987): 181–93.

———. "*Pluie et vent sur Télumée Miracle* de Simone Schwarz-Bart: Le jeu des figures répétitives dans l'oeuvre," 98–101. *Textes, Etudes et Documents.* Paris: Editions Caribéennes, 1979.

Pfaff, Françoise. *Entretiens avec Maryse Condé.* Paris: Karthala, 1993.

Philip, M. Nourbese. "Interview." With Barbara Carey. *Books in Canada* (September 1990): 17–21.

Pierre-Charles, Livie. *Femmes et chansons.* Paris: Editions Louis Soulanger, 1975.

Pieterse, J. N. *White on Black: Images of Africa and Blacks in Western Popular Culture.* New Haven: Yale University Press, 1992.

Pineau, Gisèle. "Ecrire en tant que noire." In *Penser la créolité,* ed. Maryse Condé and Madeleine Cottenet-Hage, 289–95. Paris: Karthala, 1995.

———. *La grande drive des esprits.* Paris: Le Serpent à Plumes, 1993.

———. *Un papillon dans la cité.* Paris: Sepia, 1992.

Pluchon, Pierre. *Vaudou, sorciers, empoisonneurs de Saint- Domingue à Haïti.* Paris: Karthala, 1987.

Pointer, Fritz H. "Laye, Lamming and Wright: Mother and Son." *African Literature Today* 14. London: Heinemann, 1984.

Price-Mars, Jean. *Ainsi parla l'oncle.* Ottawa: Leméac, 1973.

Ragan, Kathleen, ed. *Fearless Girls, Wise Women and Beloved Sisters: Heroines in Folktales from Around the World.* New York: W. W. Norton, 1998.

Raymond, Janice G. *A Passion for Friends: Toward a Philosophy of Female Affection.* Boston: Beacon Press, 1986.

Riesz, Janos, and Ulla Schild, ed. *Genres autobiographiques en Afrique: Actes du 6e Symposium International Janheinz Jahn/Autobiographical Genres in Africa: Papers Presented at the 6th International Janheinz Jahn Symposium (Mainz-Bayreuth 1992).* Berlin: Dietrich Reimer Verlag, 1996.

Rinne, Suzanne, and Joëlle Vitiello, eds. *Elles écrivent des Antilles: Haïti, Guadeloupe, Martinique.* Paris: L'Harmattan, 1997.

Roumain, Jacques. *Gouverneurs de la rosée.* Paris: Messidor, 1986.

Saint-Grégoire, Erma. "Interview." Trans. Mohamed B. Taleb-Khyar. *Callaloo* 15, no. 2 (1992): 462–67.

Sandin-Fremaint, Pedro A. *A Theological Reading of Four Novels by Marie Chauvet: In Search of Christic Voices.* San Francisco: Mellen Research University Press, 1992.

Scharfman, Ronnie. "Fonction romanesque féminine: Rencontre de la culture et de la structure dans *Les bouts de bois de Dieu.*" *Ethiopiques* 1, no. 3–4 (1983): 134–44.

Schipper, Mineke. *Source of All Evil: African Proverbs and Sayings on Women.* Chicago: Ivan R. Dee, 1991.

Schwarz-Bart, Simone. *Hommage à la femme noire.* 6 vols. Belgium: Editions Consulaires, 1988–89.

———. *Pluie et vent sur Télumée Miracle.* Paris: Seuil, 1972. Trans. Barbara Bray under the title *The Bridge of Beyond* (New York: Atheneum, 1974).

———. *Ton beau capitaine.* Paris: Seuil, 1987.

Schwarz-Bart, Simone, and André Schwarz-Bart. "Simone and André Schwarz-Bart: Sur les pas de Fanotte (interview)." With Héliane and Roger Toumson. In *Pluie et vent sur Télumée Miracle de Simone Schwarz-Bart,* ed. Roger Toumson. Special issue of *Textes, Etudes, Documents* 2 (1979): 13–23. Paris: Editions Caribéennes, 1979.

———. *Un plat de porc aux bananes vertes.* Paris: Seuil, 1967.

Sebastien, Joachim. *Le nègre dans le roman blanc.* Montreal: Presses de l'Université du Québec, 1980.

Sembène, Ousmane. *Les bouts de bois de Dieu.* Paris: Presses Pocket, 1960. Trans. Francis Price under the title *God's Bits of Wood* (Garden City: Doubleday, 1962).

———. *Le dernier de l'empire.* Vol. 2. Paris: L'Harmattan, 1981.

———. *L'Harmattan.* Paris: Présence Africaine, 1980.

———. *Voltaïque.* Paris: Présence Africaine, 1992. Trans. Len Ortzen under the title *Tribal Scars and Other Stories* (London: Heinemann, 1987).

———. *Xala.* Paris: Présence Africaine, 1973.

Sène, Fama Diagne. *Le chant des ténèbres.* Dakar: Nouvelles Editions du Sénégal, 1997.

Senghor, Léopold Sédar. *The Collected Poetry.* Trans. Melvin Dixon. Charlottes-ville: University Press of Virginia, 1991.

Sharp, Ronald A. *Friendship and Literature: Spirit and Form.* Durham: Duke University Press, 1986.

Shelton, Marie-Denise. "Problématique de l'espace dans l'oeuvre de Marie Chauvet." *Notre Librairie* 132 (December 1997): 142–51.

Sidibé, Mamby. *Contes populaires du Mali.* 2 vols. Paris: Présence Africaine, 1982.

Smith, Mary. *Baba of Karo: A Woman of the Moslem Hausa.* New Haven: Yale University Press, 1981.

Smith, Sidonie, and Julia Watson, eds. *De/Colonizing the Subject: The Politics of Gender in Women's Autobiography.* Minneapolis: University of Minnesota Press, 1992.

Sonfo, Alphamoye. "La mère dans la littérature romanesque de la Guinée, du Mali et du Sénégal." *Revue ouest africaine des langues vivantes* 2 (1976): 95–107.

Songue, Paulette. *Prostitution en Afrique: L'exemple de Yaoundé.* Paris: L'Harmattan, 1986.

Sow, Fatou. "Femmes, socialité et valeurs africaines." *Notes africaines* 16, no. 8 (October 1980): 105–12.

Sow Fall, Aminata. "Du pilon à la machine à écrire." *Notre Librairie* 68 (January–April 1983): 73–77.

Staunton, Irene, ed. *Mothers of the Revolution: The War Experiences of Thirty Zimbabwean Women.* Bloomington: Indiana University Press, 1991.

Steady, Filomina Chioma, ed. *The Black Woman Cross-Culturally.* Rochester, Vt.: Schenkman Books, 1985.

Stratton, Florence. *Contemporary African Literature and the Politics of Gender.* London: Routledge, 1994.

———. "'Periodic Embodiments': A Ubiquitous Trope in African Men's Writing." *Research in African Literatures* 21, no. 1 (spring 1990): 111–26.

Stringer, Susan. *The Senegalese Novel by Women: Through Their Own Eyes.* New York: Peter Lang, 1996.

Telchid, Sylviane. *Ti-Chika . . . et d'autres contes antillais.* Paris: Editions Caribéennes, 1985.

Tessonneau, Louise, ed. *Contes créoles d'Haïti.* Paris: EDICEF, 1980.

Thiam, Awa. *La parole aux négresses.* Dakar: Nouvelles Editions Africaines, 1978. Trans. Dorothy Blair under the title *Speak Out, Black Sisters: Feminism and Oppression in Black Africa* (London: Pluto, 1986).

Thoby-Marcelin, Philippe, and Pierre Marcelin. *Contes et légendes d'Haïti.* Paris: Fernand Nathan, 1967.

Todd, Janet. *Women's Friendship in Literature.* New York: Columbia University Press, 1980.

Toumson, Roger, ed. *Pluie et vent sur Télumée Miracle de Simone Schwarz-Bart.* Paris: Editions Caribéennes; Point-à-Pitre: GEREC, 1979.

Touré, Abdou. *Les petits métiers à Abidjan: L'imagination au secours de la conjoncture.* Paris: Karthala, 1985.

Toureh, Fanta. *L'imaginaire dans l'oeuvre de Simone Schwarz-Bart: Approche d'une mythologie antillaise.* Paris: L'Harmattan, 1986.

Trinh T. Minh-ha. *Woman, Native, Other: Writing, Postcoloniality and Feminism.* Bloomington: Indiana University Press, 1989.

Velayoudom Faithful, Francesca. "La femme antillaise." *Présence Africaine* 153 (1996): 112–36.

Verhaegen, Benoît. *Femmes zaïroises de Kisangani: Combats pour la survie.* Louvain-la-Neuve: Centre d'histoire de l'Afrique, Université Catholique de Louvain, 1990.

Vincent, Jeanne-Françoise. *Traditions et transition: Entretiens avec des femmes Beti du Sud-Cameroun.* Paris: ORSTOM, 1976.

Voisset, Georges M. "The 'Tebra' of Moorish Women from Mauritania: The Limits (or Essence) of the Poetic Act." *Research in African Literatures* 24, no. 2 (summer 1993): 79–88.

Volet, Jean-Marie. *La parole aux Africaines ou l'idée de pouvoir chez les romancières d'expression française de l'Afrique sub-saharienne.* Atlanta: Rodopi, 1993.

Walker, Alice. *In Search of Our Mothers' Gardens.* New York: Harcourt Brace Jovanovich, 1983.

Wall, Cheryl A., ed. *Changing Our Own Words: Essays on Criticism, Theory, and Writing by Black Women.* New Brunswick: Rutgers University Press, 1989.

Warner-Vieyra, Myriam. *Juletane.* Paris: Présence Africaine, 1982.

———. *Le quimboiseur l'avait dit.* Paris: Présence Africaine, 1980.

Washington, Mary Helen, ed. *Invented Lives: Narratives of Black Women, 1860–1960.* New York: Anchor Press, 1987.

Wilentz, Gay. *Binding Cultures: Black Women Writers in Africa and the Diaspora.* Bloomington: Indiana University Press, 1992.

Zobel, Joseph. *La rue cases-nègres.* Paris: Présence Africaine, 1974. Trans. Keith Q. Warner under the title *Black Shack Alley* (Washington, D.C., Three Continents Press, 1980).

Index

Renée Larrier is associate professor of French and is also affiliated with the Center for African Studies and the Women's Studies Department at Rutgers, the State University of New Jersey–New Brunswick. She is co-author with E. Anthony Hurley and Joseph McLaren of *Migrating Words and Worlds: Pan-Africanism Updated* and author of numerous articles on African and Caribbean literature.

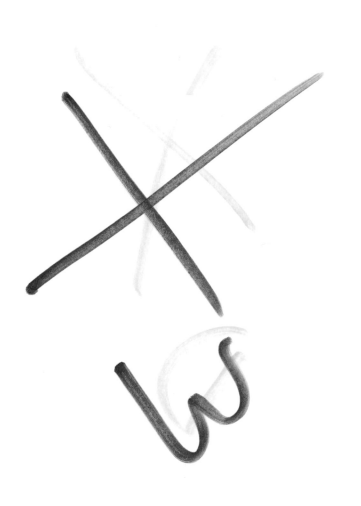